AMERICAN NEGRO SONGS

230 Folk Songs and Spirituals, Religious and Secular

JOHN W. WORK

DOVER PUBLICATIONS, INC.
Mineola, New York

Published in Canada by General Publishing Company, Ltd., 30 Lesmill Road, Don Mills, Toronto, Ontario.

Bibliographical Note

This Dover edition, first published in 1998, is an unabridged republication of the work originally published by Crown Publishers, Inc., New York, in 1940. Only the contents list has been changed, to include the Index of Song Titles.

International Standard Book Number: 0-486-40271-1

Manufactured in the United States of America
Dover Publications, Inc., 31 East 2nd Street, Mineola, N.Y. 11501

THE CONTENTS

AMERICAN NEGRO SONGS

1. ORIGINS

O I'm gonna sing, gonna sing
Gonna sing all 'long the way;
O I'm gonna sing, gonna sing,
Gonna sing all 'long the way.

THE FOLK SONG of the American Negro has not experienced the long unhindered growth common to the great body of folk songs of other people. The Negro slave from Africa was introduced into a wholly alien culture and was constantly modifying and being modified by it. In this new environment it is indeed remarkable that the Negro folk song, in such a comparatively short period of development, could retain its unique racial character and become so prolific.

It is difficult to determine the period in which Negro song first assumed a definite character in America, because there were no successful attempts to collect any Negro songs before 1840 and because early letters or articles describing Negro singing were not carefully preserved.

Music played so important a part in African life that it is natural that the Negro continued his singing after reaching America. The sorrow of his enslavement probably stirred him to sing more than he did before. It is reasonable to suppose, however, that although Negroes sang, upon reaching the shores of the new country, they did not have a uniform type of song.

Assembled, as they were, from tribes of East, West and South Africa and the interior, their customs, habits, languages, and types of music were diverse. But the general interchange of slaves among the colonies and the uniformity of social conditions partially developed and fostered by Christianity welded them into a somewhat homogeneous group, from which emerged a comparatively uniform body of song. To uncover accurate descriptions and illustrations of Negro song during this period should be a valuable aid to the study of American music.

How much of the African idiom remained in the new Negro song is hard to estimate. Complete separation of the Africans from their native land, as well as separation from individuals of the same tribe, and their sudden introduction into an alien culture, brought about an inevitable interruption of African culture in America.

Opinions among authorities vary considerably regarding the amount of African culture surviving in American Negro life. Some think it negligible. Others, including Dr. Lorenzo D. Turner, who has devoted much study to this question, particularly from the standpoint of language, contend that the survivals are extensive. Without going into a detailed discussion of this matter, it is important that reference be made to African influence and survival in the American Negro's music.

Reports of several writers present strong evidence that some African songs have persisted to this day. Edward King, in his book of Negro songs, *The Great South*, says:

> . . . . A gentleman visitor at Port Royal is said to have been struck with the resemblance of some of the tunes sung by the watermen there to boatmen's songs he had

heard on the Nile.

Marion Holland, in her *Autobiography*, relates a similar coincidence in the chapter entitled "The Old African Church," (Richmond, Virginia).

> . . . . As he sat down the audience arose as one woman and broke into a funeral chant never written in any hymn book and in which the choir who sang by note took no part:
>
> > *We'll pass over Jordan*
> > *O my brothers, O my sisters*
> > *De water's chilly and cold*
> > *But hallelujah to de Lamb;*
> > *Honor de Lamb my children,*
> > > *honor de Lamb.*

This was sung over and over with upraised arms. More than thirty years after the sermon of which I have written, our little party of American travellers drew back against the wall of the reported "house of Simon the Tanner" in Jaffa (the ancient Joppa) to let a funeral procession pass. The dead man borne without a coffin upon the shoulders of four gigantic Nubians was of their race. Two thirds of the crowd that trudged barefooted through the muddy streets behind the bier were of the same nationality, and as they plodded through the mire they chanted the identical wild, wailing measure familiar to me from infancy which was sung that Sunday afternoon to the words "We'll pass

3

over Jordan" —— even to the oft-reiterated refrain "Honor, my children, honor de Lamb." The gutterals of the outlandish tongue were all that was unlike. The air was the same and the time and intonations.

Dr. Turner relates that he learned a song on the islands off Charleston, South Carolina, which when sung before African students at the University of London was immediately familiar to them. They actually sang the song with him.

A song-form unquestionably African in origin is retained in the American Negro song. It is designated as the "call and response chant form." The "call and response" form is interesting as well as distinctive. Its feature is a melodic fragment sung repeatedly by the chorus as an answer to the challenging lines of the leader which usually change. This melodic fragment of the chorus may comprise one word, such as "Mount Zion" in the song "On Ma Journey," so well arranged by Mr. Edward Boatner; or a phrase, "For My Lord," in the song "Witness," or a sentence, "Don't You Get Weary," in the song "Great Camp Meeting."

Mrs. Merlin Ennis, a missionary in Angola, Africa, describes the natives there as singing in this same style with the chorus responding with recurring lines of words to new lines by the leader.

Dr. E. M. von Hornbostel, the eminent anthropologist, in a very enlightening article, "African Negro Music," also gives an account of the "call and response" chant form of singing by the African natives.

Henry F. Krehbiel quotes words of an African song in which every new line is answered by the line, "Oh, the broad spears." The new lines undoubtedly were sung by a leader and the answering lines by the chorus.

The collections of songs sung by Liberian natives on phonographic recordings owned by Dr. Charles S. Johnson and of those sung by Zulu natives owned by Dr. Thomas E. Jones furnish many interesting examples of this form and add further evidence that the form is African.

It will be noticed in the following examples taken from these collections that occasionally the response is identical to the call.

The genuineness and worth of the American Negro folk song and the extent to which it represents imitation of the song which surrounded it are controversial issues. Krehbiel, in the second chapter of his book *Afro-American Folk Songs*, has presented time-tested arguments of a most convincing nature that the Negro song in America is an original development. James Weldon Johnson, in the Preface to *The Book of American Negro Spirituals*, ably replies to that group of writers who disparage Negro folk-song because here and there they find traces of imitation in it! He scoffs at the idea that the Negro could have evolved "Deep River," "I Couldn't Hear Nobody Pray" and such beautiful songs from the gospel hymns he heard his white masters sing.

Dr. George Pullen Jackson of Vanderbilt University, who has devoted much time and energy to the successful development of a national appreciation of southern folk-lore, contends in his *White Spirituals in Southern Uplands*, one of the most commendable treatises on any phase of American folk-lore yet published, that the Negro spiritual is a copy of the white Gospel hymn. Other writers, notably Dr. Guy Johnson and Dr. Newman I. White, support this contention. Dr. Jackson has devoted two long chapters to the comparison of the tunes and texts of Negro and white spirituals. Many of the spirituals are nearly identical. In others striking similarities are revealed.

These similarities have confused most collectors of American Negro folk-song, but before they can be accepted as conclusive evidence that the Negro spiritual is an imitation of the white gospel song, several important factors must be considered. Among them are the Afro-American creative folk-genius, and the distinction between "imitation" and "re-assembling."

The complex rhythmic schemes of the African music, which up to the present time have defied analysis or even satisfactory description by European musicians, amply provide the Afro-American with a heredity capable of creating music as imperishable as the spiritual. These rhythmic schemes are referred to with important explanation by Krehbiel, Hornbostel and Ballanta-Taylor. While the African culture *per se* was interrupted by the African migration to America, the musicality necessary to create significant music was not disturbed. The testing of Afro-American children for inherent musicianship by Lenoire, mentioned by Mursell and again by Kwalwasser, substantiates this assertion.

In Africa native scales were purely melodic in their concept and, apparently, were composed of tones which lacked the distinct character of rest or restlessness. There is no dispute over the fact that the Africans discarded these scales when they were introducd into the new country. But the substitution of scales and tonality can hardly be construed as imitation, especially when we attach to the term "imitation" its usual connotation. It is, rather, an incorporation of free material for a distinctive use.

It is preposterous to assume that the Negro or any other group could live in an environment rich in song, and not be influenced by it. Consequently, many of the spirituals and worksongs show traces of other songs. These musically sensitive slaves made many obvious, conscious attempts to reproduce the songs they heard around them, especially the religious songs. Often the Negro sang these songs in a manner different from that in which they were sung at the camp meetings and churches, because of his insufficient acquaintance with the words and his failure to recall them accurately. But here the attempt was to reproduce rather than to imitate. Listing these inaccurate reproductions as spirituals is the error of many collectors. This fact also explains the often too similar versions of gospel songs and spirituals.

There were, however, other attitudes toward the gospel song adopted by the Negro. One of these was an unconscious criticism of the gospel hymn, which led him to re-assemble special words or phrases of interest into a *more satisfactory* musical creation. He accomplished this by translating these words or phrases into idioms, adding melodic and rhythmic motives which had already been developed and widely used by the slaves. An interesting instance of this process is "Rock of Ages." (Page 60.) The gospel hymns usually lived just a little longer than the stay of the composer-evangelist who introduced them to the community, but the spirituals were so dynamic that they spread from section to section. Today, a century after their creation, they make an enormous appeal to concert-goers in America and Europe, and their melodic and rhythmic idioms are important elements in the music America is singing.

The foregoing explains only the similarities found in what might conveniently be called the "border line" songs,—songs where sufficient question of originality gives rise to discussion. Did the gospel songs always antedate the spiritual? Where and how did Negro slave communities, far removed from any white camp meetings, evolve spirituals?

The greater number of the spirituals appear in the "call and response" chant form described above as a form peculiar to African music and as one not reproduced in any of America's music save the Negro spiritual until imitated on the minstrel stage. The fact that the bulk of the spirituals make use of this form alone eliminates grounds for the consideration of the spiritual as an imitation of the gospel hymn.

The fatal error made by many writers in this field is that in their analysis of these songs they rely altogether upon the verse, rather than upon the music. The Negro slave was too handicapped by inadequate vocabulary and too absorbed in the music to give much attention to the words. In many instances his verse was magnificent, yet throughout his songs we definitely sense the importance of music over words. He had, however, the ability to group his words into expressions that were not imitations and, in addition, defied imitation. He did not sing:

> *Praise to the living God*
> *All praised be his name*
> *Who was, and is, and is to be*
> *For aye thro' the same*
> *The one Eternal God*
> *Ere aught that now appears*
> *The first, the last, beyond all thoughts*
> *His timeless years.*

9

Instead he shortened and strengthened this by singing:

God is a God
God don't never change
God is a God
And he always will be God.

Turning again to the music, we find that there is another type of Negro song that certainly has a distinctly Afro-American character,—the *Blues*. The three-phrase form is unique; the plaintiveness of the melody and its scale are different. The proponents of the "imitation theory" must answer the question: What music in America did the Negro imitate to create the blues, or the other secular folk songs so characteristically racial?

The inferior and incongrous material found in many spirituals has resulted from the fact that these songs became so prolific within such a short period. Neither time nor sufficient contact, the two greatest known purifiers of folk-song, have had opportunity to remove this material. For instance, one person may create a song in which there are some unnatural intervals or some words that do not quite fit the meter. If the group is favorably impressed with the song as a whole, gradually, and without conscious effort, it replaces these unnatural intervals and misfit words with more suitable ones. Thus, in the course of time this song as it spreads over the country becomes unconsciously perfected and standardized. Examples of this process are "Swing Low Sweet Chariot," "Steal Away to Jesus," "Lord, I Want to Be a Christian," and "Go Down Moses."

So, when one hears an incidental song or verse in a song which seems queer, artificial or unpoetic, a test should be made to ascertain whether it is folk or individual, by determining the frequency with which it is encountered in other communities.

In a community in which I lived one summer, one man invariably sang this verse with almost every song he led:

> 'Way over yonder on Jericho's wall
> I thought I hyeard an angel squall.

I never heard it sung by anyone else or anywhere else. Recently a Fisk student gave me this verse which he had heard in a church service just out of Corinth, Mississippi:

> Snuff and tobacco you'd better quit,
> 'When you get to heab'n there'll be no place to spit,
> I know the Bible right, I know the Bible right
> No termdemnation, no termdemnation in my heart.

Obviously this verse would not become very widespread. Again, the following verse would hardly be sung in many churches:

> Wait till I get upon the mountain top
> Goin' make my wings go flippity-flop.

Faulty hearing and faulty memory also figure prominently in the amount of error found in these songs. A song sung in Georgia and then heard in Tennessee or Texas may not be recognized as the same song because of the amount of error in melody and words introduced by the imperfect carrier. Thus we have two versions of "Swing Low Sweet Chariot," "Were You There When They Crucified My Lord?" and "I Am So Glad." One of the leading singers in a student organization at Fisk University had been sounding a bit different from the rest of the group when they were singing "The Ol' Ark's a-Mover-in'." Upon listening very carefully to him I was both surprised and amused to find that he was singing "Whole Lot's a-Moverin'." He had sung it in that way all of his life.

Dr. Newman I. White, in his book *American Negro Folk Songs,* makes the assertion that spirituals are the result of exploitation by slave-holders who had found that the slaves worked better under the influence of songs of a certain type, and who therefore fashioned, in many instances, the songs they wished the slaves to sing. He tells of the concern about and the opposition toward the christianizing of the slaves which the slaveholders in general manifested. Some said that religion demoralized the slaves.

Yet, almost the entire body of slave songs that has been collected is made up of the religious folksongs. Such coercion must have been a negligible element in the origin of a body of song of which one of the most apparent features is spontaneity. Moreover, the slave-holder must have forbidden a considerable number of spirituals which clothed in the highest imagery the burdens of slavery and inevitable deliverance.

Dr. White's assertion appears untenable when we consider such songs as these, which are very numerous: "Steal Away to Jesus," "Nobody Knows the Trouble I See, Glory Hallelujah!", "Before I'd Be a Slave I'd Be Buried in My Grave," "Nobody Knows Who I am," "Who Will Deliver Po' Me," "Walk Together Children, Don't You Get Weary," "Children We Shall Be Free," "I'm a-Rolling Through an Unfriendly World," "Didn't My Lord Deliver Daniel?", "Go Down Moses," "Keep Me from Sinking Down," "Many Thousand Gone," "My Way's Cloudy," and "Don't You Grieve after Me."

Year by year the number of new folk-songs seems to diminish. It is possible that the type of folk-song designated in the collection as "social" has disappeared, as its function has been more efficiently performed by music of a different sort. The work song, too, has all but passed. The *blues*, while not produced in the large numbers of twenty years ago, still hold a popular place with the Negro singer. Such great songs as "Little Low Mamma Blues," and "Back Water Blues," substantiate the belief that the blues strain is still fertile enough to produce some still greater songs. Yet the spiritual goes on showing the strength of its strain. The Reverend Zema Hill, of the Primitive Baptist Church at Nashville, Tennessee, composes new spirituals of sound merit, which attract huge crowds to his services.

This song, in which the influence of passing events on Negro folk-song is clearly shown, was heard recently in Huntsville, Alabama.

2. THE SPIRITUAL

Lord, I want to be a Christian
In my heart, in-a my heart
Lord, I want to be a Christian
In-a my heart.

THE largest number of Negro folk-songs collected thus far are spirituals. They were first presented to the world at large by the Fisk Jubilee Singers, who toured America and Europe from 1871 to 1878. The story of these singers—their organization and tours—is a fascinating and heroic one, and is so closely connected with the development of America's interest in the spirituals that it seems appropriate to relate a part of it.

Fisk University was established in 1866 for freedmen by northern educational interests, as were so many of the schools for Negroes which were established in the South after the Civil War. Shortly after its founding many unforeseen problems arose to perplex the administration. The gravest of these was the problem of funds to carry forward the work of the school. The lack of money produced such a precarious situation that it seemed inevitable that Fisk must close its doors.

The treasurer of the school, Mr. George L. White, had listened with keen interest to the singing of the students, and in a moment of inspiration stated his belief that if the world could hear these strange songs it would experience the same exaltation which he felt when listening to them, and somehow, out of this, sufficient interest could be aroused to help the new educational experiment. He gained the reluctant permission of the authorities to undertake the organization of a group of students into a chorus, with the purpose of making a concert tour.

Excellent voices were abundant among the students. From these Mr. White selected twelve and began more than two years of intensive training.

The type of program to be offered presented several problems of large proportions. America had seen Negroes on the stage before—but they were minstrels. Was America prepared to receive Negroes on the stage in a serious role? What could these young people offer that would interest America and at the same time be worthy of a college? By what name should they be known?

Mr. White decided on a style of singing the spiritual which eliminated every element that detracted from the pure emotion of the song. Harmony was diatonic and limited very largely to the primary triads and the dominant seventh. Dialect was not stressed but was used only where it was vital to the spirit of the song. Finish, precision, and sincerity were demanded by this leader. While the program featured the spirituals, variety was given it by the use of numbers of classical standard. Mr. White strove for an art presentation, not a caricature of atmosphere.

At last the singers were ready. They left Nashville on October sixth, 1871. During the first part of the tour Mr. White gave the group the inspired name, "The Jubilee Singers," and called their music "Jubilee Songs."

At first America did not know how to receive the Jubilee Singers. Its first attitude was one of indifference and derision. There soon developed, however, an enthusiasm which led the singers to heights of success far beyond their hopes.

After a successful tour of America, a smaller company of eight singers were taken to Europe where they scored a triumph. They sang before the crowned heads and were entertained by Gladstone and the Earl of Shaftsbury. The latter was their most enthusiastic patron. Describing their singing, Mr. Colin Brown, Ewing Lecturer on Music, Anderson University at Glasgow, wrote:

> As to the manner of their singing it must be heard before it can be realized. Like the Swedish melodies of Jennie Lind, it gives a new musical idea. It has been well remarked that in some respects it disarms criticism, in others it may be truly said that it almost defies it. It was beautifully described by a simple Highland girl —"It filled my whole heart." Such singing (in which the artistic is lost in the natural) can only be the result of the most careful training. The richness and purity of tone, both in melody and harmony, the contrast of light and shade, and the exquisite refinement of the piano as contrasted with the power of the forte, fill us with delight, and at the same time make us feel how strange it is that these unpretending singers should come over here to teach us what is the true refinement of music, make us feel its moral and religious power.

In 1878 the Singers returned to Fisk with more than one hundred and fifty thousand dollars. Just as important as this money, however, was the interest the Jubilee Singers had created over the world in Negro education and in the spirituals, known until recently by the name they gave them—Jubilee Songs.

In 1824, a colony of about two hundred freedmen from Kentucky, Pennsylvania and South Carolina was organized at Samana Bay under the Haitian Republic. This colony voluntarily remained isolated from the surrounding islanders and thus preserved its dialect. These colonists no longer sing the spirituals in their church services but they use them at their parties for corn huskings.

Recently a church gathering sang for visitors some spirituals that are very familiar in this country,—among them was "Roll Jordan Roll."

This is important. Since this colony has existed in comparative isolation, the singing of spirituals is significant. If "Roll Jordan Roll" was taken to this colony in 1824 in the state in which it now exists in America, it must have been generally known. The number of years before 1824 which it must have taken first for the process of unconscious perfection and standardization, the development cycle discussed in the preceeding chapter, and, second, for the extremely gradual dissemination of the spiritual over widely separated sections of the country would unquestionably lead us to the possibility that "Roll Jordan Roll" is an eighteenth century creation.

Frequently today, but quite generally before and during the Reconstruction Period, the spiritual functioned in two ways other than religious expression. It served as the work song and as the social song. However, any spiritual which was used generally as a work song or a social song soon lost its religious significance. It is probable that the spirituals we trace in part in the early minstrel songs are those which had thus degenerated.

Many grand songs have been eschewed by the church because they had been used too commonly in non-religious activities. One typical example of this is the spiritual "Wasn't That a Mighty Day when Jesus Christ was Born," majestic in melodic line as well as in word. It was used and still is used by minstrel quartets who feature it with some ridiculous cadenzas for the bass singer.

So strong were the demands of the Negro church upon a member that he was forced to refrain from singing all songs of a secular nature. But, the Negro, compelled by nature to sing as he worked, had to sing religious songs. Frequently, in my search for songs I have found it impossible to persuade church members to sing a work song or a social song for me, because it was "sinful." The church placed the same ban on secular songs in entertainments and suppers that it sponsored.

To this day in the rural sections one of the features of amusement of a party given by the church or its members is a spirited circular march by couples, the music for which is a very highly rhythmic spiritual. At one of these parties which I attended a few years ago the people were marching to "Hammering," one of the most gripping crucifixion spirituals yet discovered.

From the standpoint of form, melodic variety, and emotional expressiveness, the spiritual is the most highly developed of the Negro folk-songs. There are many types of spirituals, but they can be classed in three groups: the "call and response chant"; the slow, sustained, long-phrase melody; and the syncopated, segmented melody.

In the first main type we find such songs as "Great Camp Meeting," "Shout for Joy," "Good Morning Everybody," "Swing Low Sweet Chariot," and "Sittin' Down beside the Lamb." The largest number of spirituals, and possibly the most interesting ones, embrace this form. These songs are sung in a rapid tempo, and are characterized by fiery spirit. The calmness of "Swing Low Sweet Chariot" is an exception.

The second type of spiritual includes such songs as "Deep River," "Nobody Knows the Trouble I see," "My Lord What a Morning," and "Were You There?" Several noteworthy characteristics are discernible from an analysis of these spirituals. The tempo of songs in this class is slow and the phrase line long and sustained. Usually the words make long phrases or complete sentences. Fewer songs are known in this mold than in the others. In the spirituals created today this type is rare.

In the third class of spiritual we find the songs which probably are the most popular, such as "Shout All over God's Heab'n," "Little David Play on Yo' Harp," "Ain't Goin' to Study War no Mo," and "Ol' Ark's a-Moverin'." The tempo of these songs is usually fast and the rhythm features a swing which stimulates bodily movement. The musical line instead of being a complete, sustained phrase is often made up of segments or rhythmic patterns with a syncopated figure. As is to be expected the words are usually in short phrase length, or one repeated word, rather than in complete lines as are found in "Were You There?" and songs of its class.

A prominent characteristic of this type of spiritual is a repeated, short rhythmic-pattern usually syncopated, but if not syncopated, featuring an important pulse note. There is frequently an unusual distribution of notes within the pattern.

The following are four typical ones:

Alteration of these rhythmic patterns is not allowed. This inviolability of the rhythmic pattern in the spiritual illustrates the interesting fundamental principle of the importance of note over word. To the singers the music was the significant factor, with the words occupying a secondary role, even though their meaning was often sacrificed.

In one of the patterns illustrated above, "Ain't you Glad You Got Good Religion," the least important word in the phrase is given the most prominent rhythmic pulse. The fact that the same faulty (to our ears) prosody occurred throughout the song did not disturb the singers at all.

Again, in the song "I've Found Free Grace and Dying Love," we note that the statement is obviously the opposite to the intended meaning. In the rhythmic pattern allowance was made for one syllable when originally there were two in the word-phrase— ". . . an' *Un*dying Love." One of these must be omitted. Unfortunately, as a result the important qualifying syllable "un" was sacrificed in favor of the unimportant "an'."

A variant of this principle appears in the chronicle of Methuselah's life. He is described in the Bible as having lived nine hundred and sixty-nine years. But in relating it in the spiritual the singers added thirty years to his life because they could sing "ninety" more pleasingly than "sixty." So we have this story:

> *We read in the Bible an' we understan'*
> *Methuselah was the oldes' man,*
> *He lived nine hundred and ninty-nine*
> *He died an' went to heaven, Lord, in-a due time.*

There is no necessity to imagine that the expressed words represent any confusion in the minds of the creators. The changes can be explained by recognizing the creators' unconscious effort to produce perfect music, with the obvious meaning of the words left to the common knowledge or feeling of the listeners.

These statements must not be construed to mean that much importance was not placed on the words of the spiritual. True, the conflict of the word-phrase with the rhythmic figure resulted in the seeming distortion of the former, but the conflicts were not frequent. The verse of the spirituals was distinctive and showed a rare skill on the part of the poets to relate events or moods in an inimitable style, making almost every line a unique expression.

Observe a few first-lines: "Roll, Jordan, Roll," "O po' sinner what you goin' to do when yo' lamp burns down?" "Done made my vow to the Lord an' I never will turn back," "Oh sinner, please

21

don't let this harves' pass," "Keep a-inchin' along Jesus'll come bye 'n' bye," and "My Lord what a mournin' when the stars begin to fall."

The Negro bard has in his verse almost completely reconstructed the most important events in the Bible. In his songs he has chronicled them in such a way as to defy imitation. Illustrations of these are:

We read in the Bible and we understan'
That Samson was the strongest man
Samson went out at one time
And killed about a thousand Philistines.
Delilah fooled Samson, this we know
Because the Holy Bible tells us so.
She shaved off his head just as clean as your han',
And his strength became as any other man.

I heard a mighty rumbling under the groun'
It must be the devil running aroun'.
I heard a mighty rumbling up in the sky
It must be Jehovah passing by.
Jehovah sent down His chariot of fire
and carried Elijah up higher and higher.

Daniel was a Hebrew child
He went to pray to his God for a while
The King at once for Daniel did sen'
And he put him right down in the lion's den,
The Lord sent His angels the lions for to keep
And Daniel lay down and he went to sleep.

For the slave there was only one religion. He remembered no other. There were in his philosophy of life two possible ways of living, and he must choose one. Either he must join the church and dream and sing of the pearly gates, the golden streets, the long white robe, the starry crown and everlasting happiness, or stay outside the fold and risk the terrors of the eternal companionship of Satan. He usually joined the church. How could he refrain from so doing with such verses as these ringing in his ears?

> *Ol' Satan's got a slippery ol' shoe*
> *And if you don't mind he will slip it on you.*
>
> *Ol' Satan's like a snake in the grass*
> *Waitin' to bite you as you pass.*
>
> *Never mind what ol' Satan may say*
> *He never taught one soul to pray.*
>
> *Shout! shout! Satan's about*
> *Shut yo' do' and keep him out.*
>
> *Ol' Satan's mad and I am glad*
> *He missed the soul he thought he had.*

His religion, however, was divided into two spiritually militant groups, Methodists and Baptists, and the spirit was so bitter between them that social separation frequently resulted. Being a Methodist was sufficient reason for a Baptist to disdain friendship. And so they sang of this. The Methodist sang:

> *There's a camp meeting in the wilderness*
> *I know it's among the Methodes'.*

My father says it is bes'
To live and die a Methodes'.

The Baptist, not to be outdone, sang:

I'm Baptis' bred and Baptis' bo'n,
And when I'm dead there's a Baptis' gone.

Denominational strife continues in these verses with the Baptist scoring a signal triumph:

'Twas at the river Jordan
Baptism was begun
John baptized a multitude
But he sprinkled nary a-one.

Evidently he felt a tinge of pity for his Methodist brother, for he immediately added this verse as a balm:

The Baptists they go by water
The Methodists they go by lan'
But when they get to heaven
They'll shake each other's han'.

In my opinion these black singers reached the pinnacle of noble expressiveness, and dramatic description in their tragic, beautiful, poignant portrayal of the crucifixion. "Hammering," "Were you there," "Calvary," "They led my Lord Away," and "He never said a mumblin' word" are all unforgettable versions. This song is very graphic:

The angels done bowed down
The angels done bowed down

The angels done bowed down
The angels done bowed down

While Jesus was hanging upon the cross,
The angels kept quiet till God went off.
The angels hung their harps on the willow trees,
To give satisfaction till God was pleased.

His soul went up on a piller of cloud,
God He moved an' the heavens did bow
Jehovah's sword was at His side,
On the empty air He began to ride.

Go down angels to the flood,
Blow out the sun turn the moon into blood!
Come back angels bolt the door,
Because the time that's been goin' to be no more.

The angels done bowed down
The angels done bowed down.

With all the works of beautiful Christmas carols, the creations of those illiterate but inspired men must take their place in the front rank. Consider the simple beauty, the tenderness, and the adoration of this opening line of "Glory to that New-Born King," "O Mary, what you goin' to name that pretty little baby?" Consider the majesty of that paean, "Wasn't that a mighty day when Jesus Christ was born!"

There is a certain elusive quality heard in the native singing of the melodies that defies musical notation. For lack of suitable symbols, it is impossible to record on paper many of these songs as they are sung in their native environment. Extravagant postamenta, slurs, and free use of extra notes serve to mystify the collector of these songs who strives for accuracy.

Of much interest are the scales of the Negro employed in the spirituals. He unconsciously avoided the fourth and seventh major scale steps in many songs, thereby using the pentatonic scale. But there were employed notes foreign to the conventional major and minor scales with such frequency as to justify their being regarded as distinct. The most common of these are the "flatted third" (the feature note of the blues) and the "flatted seventh."

The latter note is seen prominently in the songs "Roll Jordan Roll," "Soon-a Will Be Done," (second tune), "Great Camp Meeting," and "Wish I's in Heab'n Settin' Down." The scale employed in "You May Bury me in the East" corresponds closely to the Dorian mode. Several songs make use of the Phrygian mode. "Lord Help the Po' and Needy" is one.

Although the spirituals usually lend themselves readily to four-part harmony, and concert singers have sung them with varied tempos and dynamics quite effectively, nevertheless, in the rural churches from where they mostly spring they are sung with a minimum of such modifications. There are few contrasting passages such as loud and soft; no notes are held for effect longer than the pulse indicates; and strangest of all, there are no retards to anticipate the closing cadence. The leader establishes his tempo and maintains it throughout the song. Harmony occasionally is in two parts, rarely in three. I have never encountered four-part harmony.

The leader is a most important factor in the singing of spirituals. It is he who sets the pitch and tempo, and it is he who sings the verses. The leader sometimes must sing his refrain through several times before the group will join him. He must have at his disposal many verses for each song.

Many churches have spirituals which are led exclusively by special singers. Thus, within a church a spiritual may be designated as "Brother Jones' song," or "Sister Mary's song." Such songs may have been composed, or merely introduced into the church singing by the leader. The "ownership" of such a song carried with it the indisputable ability to sing it effectively. In this manner traditions of singing grew around certain spirituals. It was not unusual that a song ceased to be sung in a church after a famous leader of it had died.

The spirituals in this collection represent more than a half century of collecting. "Jubilees" sung by the original Fisk Jubilee Singers are included as are spirituals gathered in the past year.

3. THE BLUES

Woke up dis mornin' feelin' sad an' blue
Woke up dis mornin' feelin' sad an' blue
Didn't have nobody to tell my troubles to.

THE BLUES DIFFER radically from the spirituals. The spirituals are choral and communal, the blues are solo and individual. The spirituals are intensely religious, and the blues are just as intensely worldly. The spirituals sing of heaven, and of the fervent hope that after death the singer may enjoy the celestial joys to be found there. The blues singer has no interest in heaven, and not much hope in earth—a thoroughly disillusioned individual. The spirituals were created in the church; the blues sprang from everyday life. The exalted verse of many spirituals could be read appropriately from the most dignified pulpit, while most of the verse of the blues is unprintable. The spirituals were created and performed without instrumental accompaniment, but the guitar, piano, or orchestral accompaniment is an integral part of the performance of the blues. Again the spiritual creators thought of every happening in nature as epic—some dispensation from God or a message from him. The blues singer translated every happening into his own intimate inconvenience. To the spiritual creators, the great Mississippi flood of a few years ago would have been considered a visitation of a wrathful God upon a sinful community. To a blues singer it simply raised the question, "Where can a po' girl go?"

Until the recent extensive commercialization of the blues by the phonograph companies and the jazz bands, these songs were the creations of nameless individuals who coined them out of experiences fraught with disillusionment, disappointment, and hopelessness. After the creation of these songs, however inspired by some very recent predicament or impending one, which creation in most instances is spontaneous, they are taken over by the folk as their unquestioned possession. It is common to hear blues sung now that were played a few years ago on phonograph records.

The phonograph recording of these songs does not destroy their "folkness." The same person who formerly created the blues for her own use and the entertainment of her immediate audience, now creates them for phonograph recordings, and justifiably so. Now a new blues may be heard in all sections of the country in the short period of a month or less after the issuing of the record, whereas formerly it probably took years for one to become known and sung generally. An interesting observation of this fact is that in the process of "taking over" of a blues by the folk, the individual singing it almost always gives her own coloring to the song by modifying, omitting, and adding lines.

The sentiments expressed in these songs are generally sad and sorrowful, even if interspersed with bits of humor. They embrace narrative and philosophical versions of disillusioned love affairs, general dissatisfaction and misfortune. Some typical blues verse follows:

Sometimes I feel like nothin', somethin' th'owed away
Sometimes I feel like nothin', somethin' th'owed away
Then I get my guitar and play the blues all day.

Money's all gone, I'm so far from home
Money's all gone, I'm so far from home
I just sit here and cry and moan.

I smell your bread a-burnin', turn yo' damper down.
I smell your bread a-burnin', turn yo' damper down.

When a woman gets the blues she hangs her head and cries,
When a woman gets the blues she hangs her head and cries,
When a man gets the blues, he catches a train and rides.

Good lookin' woman make a bull dog break his chain,
Good lookin' woman make a bull dog break his chain,
Good lookin' woman make a snail catch a passenger train.

Yaller gal make a preacher lay his Bible down,
Yaller gal make a preacher lay his Bible down
Good lookin' high brown make him run from town to town.

Good lookin' woman make a mule kick his stable down
Good lookin' woman make a mule kick his stable down
Good lookin' woman make a rabbit move his family to town.

Bo weevil don't sing dem blues no mo'
Bo weevil don't sing dem blues no mo'
Bo weevil here, bo weevil everywhere you go.

Seems like every minute goin' to be my last,
Seems like every minute goin' to be my last,
If I can't tell my future, I won't tell my past.

The leaves on the trees, oh the leaves on the trees fallin' down,

The leaves on the trees, oh the leaves on the trees fallin' down,
You left me down on my knees crawlin' round.

Woman without a man like a ship without a sail
Woman without a man like a ship without a sail
Ship without a sail like a dog without a tail.

If you didn't want me girlie what made you say you do
If you didn't want me girlie what made you say you do
Take your time little girl, nobody's rushin' you.

I may act funny, I may walk crooked, lie crossways in my bed,
I may act funny, I may walk crooked, lie crossways in my bed,
You'd better stop rockin', you heard what papa said.

Goin' up the country, sorry I can't carry you,
Goin' up the country, sorry I can't carry you,
Nothin' up the country a good girl can do.

Oh! I ain't going to tell you no mo',
Oh! I ain't going to tell you no mo',
Knock on my front window, don't knock at my back do'.

I'm awful lonesome, all alone and blue
I'm awful lonesome, all alone and blue
Ain't got nobody to tell my troubles to.

Undoubtedly the outstanding figure associated with the blues is W. C. Handy. It was he who caught the spirit of this new musical form, translated it into a new dance vehicle and first presented it successfully to America's dance floors and concert halls. The book, *Blues: An Anthology*, edited by Mr. Handy, contains an exhaustive treatise on the subject by Mr. Abbe Niles, written largely from inter-views with Mr. Handy. Mr. Handy's many compositions for the dance are a vital part of popular music today, and they include several songs with a quality that makes for long, enduring popularity, notably, the *Memphis Blues*, published in 1912, and the *St. Louis Blues*, published in 1914.

Several sections of Mr. Handy's book consider the origin of this interesting body of song, and a careful reading of these sections makes it seem safe to consider the blues a twentieth century product, mak-ing their appearance about 1900. Handy first heard them in 1903.

"Ma" Rainey heard them in 1902 in a small town in Missouri where she was appearing with a show under a tent. She tells of a girl from the town who came to the tent one morning and began to sing about the "man" who had left her. The song was so strange and poignant that it attracted much attention. "Ma" Rainey became so interested that she learned the song from the visitor, and used it soon afterwards in her "act" as an encore.

The song elicited such response from the audiences that it won a special place in her act. Many times she was asked what kind of song it was, and one day she replied, in a moment of inspiration, "It's the *Blues*."

That is what "Ma" Rainey said when she allowed me to interview her in the Douglass Hotel in Nashville, where her company was play-ing. She added that a fire destroyed some newspaper clippings which mentioned her singing of these strange songs in 1905. She added, however, that after she began to sing the blues, although they were not so named then, she frequently heard similar songs in the course of her travels.

"Ma" Rainey is an interesting woman with a picturesque stage appearance, a deep contralto voice, and an authentic manner of singing the blues. She must be regarded as one of the most famous blues singers who has appeared on the stage.

The ordinary folk-song form is, of course, in two parts, generally spoken of as *verse* and *chorus*, but the form of the blues is unusual, displaying a three phrase part form, with phrase *A* the statement, *B*, repetition of the words with a variation of melody, and *C*, the consequent phrase with contrasted melody, and almost always a new line of words. The following example is typical.

If you don't be-lieve I'm sinkin'___ look what a hole I'm in,

If you don't believe I love you___ look what a hole I'm in,

If you don't believe I love you___ look what a fool I've been.

Here it must be stated that there is a distinction between the folk-blues and compositions in folk-blues form with which this discussion concerns itself, and its off-spring, a strictly commercial type of song which bears the name "Blues." This latter song is expanded in form and has a radically different style. We have examples of this in "The Limehouse Blues," "Broadway Blues," "Alcoholic Blues," "Blue Danube Blues," and "Florida Blues."

Since the "blue note" was discussed in the chapter on Spirituals, the tonality of the blues will only be touched upon here. It is sufficient to repeat that the "blue note," the flatted or diminished third of the major key is a very frequent one in the blues, although it must be noticed that a large number of blues examined do not have it The flatted seventh is used effectively also.

A check on fifty blues on phonograph records and eighteen others sung and played by George Gibson and Earl Woodward shows the following results:

Flatted third and Flatted seventh	Flatted third	Flatted seventh	Neither
14	17	29	8

The origin of the blues is generally associated with the many social songs used by the Negroes at their dances and parties. The peculiar idiomatic tonality of the songs is traced to the "holler," a fragmentary bit of yodel, half sung, half yelled, by which the Negro was known all over the country side. Approaching his house or that of his sweetheart in the evening, or sometimes out of sheer lonesomeness, he would emit his "holler." Listeners would say, "Here comes Sam," or "Will Jackson's coming," or "I just heard Archie down the road." Most of these "hollers" can be written down, although very roughly. In trying to collect some "hollers," I found the young men famous for them so bashful or self-conscious that they either disclaimed any knowledge or were unable to reproduce them satisfactorily. But I had several older people reproduce "hollers" that they remembered, and I list some I have thus received.

In these "hollers" the idiomatic material found in the blues is readily seen; the excessive portament, the slow time, the preference for the flatted third, the melancholy type of tune, the characteristic cadence. As a matter of fact, with a little more formal arrangement many of these "hollers" could serve as lines of blues.

Of inestimable help to me in this study have been George Gibson and Earl Woodard, two musicians thoroughly steeped in the lore of blues and other folk dance music, and endowed with fine musical sensitiveness.

George Gibson, genial young man, is always ready to play his fiddle for anyone who asks it. It is hard to place the source of the powerful musical inspiration which grips him. He knows no notes when he sees them, but knows them all when he hears them. He possesses absolute pitch, and his ear is the only instrument he uses in tuning his fiddle. He says that he cannot "make music" and work, and so his only livelihood is his earnings from the dances for which he can play. These are not frequent but he is happy with his fiddle.

Earl Woodard is a rock-mason, and he works at that trade whenever he cannot find Gibson. His instrument is the guitar, and he is known as "the best guitar player in South Nashville," a reputation he guards most jealously.

My first meeting with these men was an unforgettable one. It was in the back room of a shanty where Gibson lived. One cold January afternoon they played blues for me—blues I had never heard before nor since. Most of the blues they played and sang were their own creations, and I rather suspect that one or two or more were composed at the sitting, judging from the smiles of evident pleasure that enveloped their faces at the singing of certain lines.

After they had played three or four stanzas of a given song, one of them would start singing. When he was near the end of his immediate supply of verses he would sing directly to the other one, who would then take the song up and sing until all of his verses were at an end. At this point he would in the same manner signal the first singer who was now ready with a new supply of verses recalled and some probably composed. This would continue indefinitely until one of them would sing this verse which closed most of their songs:

> *If anybody ask you who composed this song,*
> *If anybody ask you who composed this song,*
> *Tell 'em sweet papa Gibson (or Woodard)*
> *Jes gone 'long.*

4. WORK SONGS

Captain, Captain, you must be cross
It's six o'clock an' you won't knock off!

THE WORK SONGS of the Negro form a clear reflection of his life during Reconstruction days. They portray vividly the conditions under which he found himself living and working. The Spirituals reflect the intense religious life that the ante-bellum Negro experienced, but they reveal little of his everyday experiences. Since most experience had religious significance, it was immediately expressed in religious music. But the social songs supplement the expression on a more homely, realistic plane.

Reconstruction brought perilous times to the Negro. Working conditions had been revolutionized. At first there was very little uniformity in these conditions, except the uniformity of long hours. The working hours of the Negro of that period are described by the old expression which he coined, "I works from *kin* to *can't*,—from the time I first kin see till I can't see." We also see the unfavorableness of another feature of his working conditions—uncertain pay—in the following song:

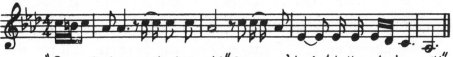

"O Captain, my han's is cold." Doggone yo' han's, let the wheeler roll!"
"O Captain has de money come? 'Tain't none o'yo' bizness I don't owe you none!

Negro laborers usually sang while working, but aside from the pleasure they received from this activity the singing had at times a definite function for them—that of coordinating their efforts. In ordinary labor any song would suffice, and for the most part they sang spirituals; but for certain types of work where rhythmic group action made the work easier a special type of song became necessary. When the group was "whippin' steel," "hammerin'," or "drillin'," the work was co-ordinated by one of these songs sung by a leader only.

In ordinary labor the whole group might sing, but in the special kinds only the leader sang. The leader was not chosen haphazardly, but was a specialist. He had to know the work thoroughly, had to know rhythm, and he had to coordinate these effectively by selecting the appropriate song. He made the work easier and through his choice of subjects entertained his gang at the same time. He was an important person in the work organization. We read frequently of his value to the "boss" and how much greater the amount of work he caused the gang to accomplish for the "boss"; but he was just as valuable to the gang and just as highly appreciated by them.

The Reverend Israel Golphin tells of his employment with a gang laying railroad tracks in Arkansas because he was a good singer. He had just asked the "boss-man" for work and had been refused. He watched the gang work for a while and noticed that they were in difficulty because the singer or "caller," as he is sometimes termed, was inexperienced and was timing them wrongly. The men were grumbling. Golphin offered to "call" for them. The gang so appreciated him that they went to the "boss-man" and requested that he be hired—and he was.

Although the Negro's work songs covered many subjects, apparently he was most fond of singing about men who were heroes in his eyes; and the hero who gripped his imagination more than any other was John Henry, the "steel drivin' man."

John Henry was engaged in the construction of the Big Ten tunnel in West Virginia, according to one of the famous stories about him. He was the most famous steel driver and driller of all the workers there. The hammer he used was much bigger than that used by the other "drivers." The "steel driver" was the highest class of workman there and, justly, he was a very proud person. Often among the drivers there were contests to decide who could drill the deepest in a given time. John Henry won all such contests.

One day an agent came to the tunnel with a steam drill and demonstrated it. This machine excited John Henry's ire and contempt, and he challenged the agent to an all day drilling contest between himself and the steam drill. The challenge was accepted. The whole country-side heard of the impending contest and was on hand to witness it.

The contest was a grim and heroic one and out of it John Henry and his hammer emerged immortal. At the close of the contest it was found that John Henry had drilled eighteen inches deeper than the steam drill—but he fell dead.

There are almost as many versions of this story as there are narrators and singers, and consequently many believe the story to be only a legend. Professor Guy B. Johnson of the University of North Carolina undertook to trace the story, and the results of his search are to be found in his book, *John Henry*. He was unable to prove any of the stories definitely true. Neither was he able to find the time or place in which the contest was staged, or anyone who could truthfully say that he knew or had seen John Henry.

However, John Henry and his hammer are heroic realities in the mind of the Negro workmen; and they sing more of him than of any other character or subject. Most of the work songs about John Henry are hammer songs, though the narrative song which tells most about this famous character is a social song.

Lazarus is another character much sung about, although he is the object of pity.

The men sang another type of song when they were not engaged in group efforts, but were working at individual tasks. This song was a solo affair whose melody had little significance. It was little more than intonation, although the two lines possessed a semi-cadence and cadence as well as a climax note. The song was not sung for the group's benefit usually, but was the singer's soliloquy on the trivialities of life as they directly affected him. Its verse was subjective, just as that of the blues, though probably not so poignant. It was also in two lines rather than three.

Sometimes the lines of the song were intended for someone other than the laborer himself. Frequently there was a thought he wished to convey to the "boss." He knew from experience that he could sing at the boss things which he could not say to him safely. The verse heading this chapter is typical. The following are a few characteristic verses found in these songs:

I asked the captain "what time o'day?"
He got so mad he jes' walked away.
Captain says "hurry"! Straw boss says "run."
I got a good notion not to do nar' one.
Befo' I'd drive a six-mule team
I'd drink my water from a runnin' stream.

5. Social and Miscellaneous Songs

THE social song was used for dancing and was generally sung by the players. When work gangs assembled in camps at the close of their day's work they passed the hours before bedtime in singing and playing. The songs sung on these occasions were generally the same as those played at parties and dances.

While the spirituals in their natural setting were rarely sung with instrumental accompaniment, and the work songs in their setting never, the social song was primarily instrumental, with the words merely incidental. In contrast to the spirituals which were choral, the social song was a solo performance, but one where quality of voice was of little consequence since the success of the entertainer depended upon his ingenuity in developing and embellishing his accompaniment.

In the creation of all Negro folk songs, improvisation plays an important part and it is an art developed very highly by all the successful performers. In this function improvisation may be described as the practice of adapting readily previously assembled common idioms.

Listening to authentic performances of these songs, or to records of folk blues, reveals that while the singer and accompanist are in perfect accord, each succeeding verse of the song is a variation of the music of the first—an employment of different idioms. The variations are usually spontaneously conceived. The written note is unthought of. The larger the supply and the more complex the idioms the more interesting is the performance. These idioms are both vocal and in-strumental. It is the use of these usually unwritten vocal idioms by a concert artist which makes the listeners decide whether or not the performance of a spiritual is authentic. The idiomatic material is so characteristic that when it appears in art compositions it usually is easily detectable.

The facility with which the creators improvise arises in the wealth of embellishment figures and devices these musicians have at their command. Tricks of embellishment, originally the property of one player, once exhibited, become the property of all players who hear him. Thus there were certain rudimentary devices of accompaniment taught or "picked up" by the beginner in piano-playing, that were used all over the South, and a consequent development of a folk style among the Southern instrumentalists resulted.

The social songs covered many subjects and moods, which ranged from heroic characters and events of national importance to the most trivial things. The life and death of notorious characters fired the imagination of many song-makers. The individual flaunting the law served to appeal much more to the creators than did those of better social status.

In the spiritual we hear the singer glorifying his preacher, his elder, and deacon. He was always wishing to meet his "dear old elder" in heaven. But in the social songs little mention was made of the preacher or churchman except in a derogatory manner, as shown by the lines:

> *Some folks say a preacher won't steal,*
> *I caught two in my corn field.*

The boat races up and down the Mississippi were subjects for some of the songs and, peculiarly, the *Titanic* disaster was the subject of much verse contained in these songs.

As expressed in another chapter, the social folk song is rapidly passing out of existence. Certainly, very few, if any, are being created, and there are few occasions for their performance at all. The jazz band and the phonograph started the declining popularity of these songs, and now the radio is completing it. The popular dance songs of today, through the modern musical organizations, serve the needs of the revelers much more completely than the old folk song did.

As much regretted as the decline of this body of song is the passing of the musical organizations so closely associated with it—the string bands. The string-band was made up of a fiddle (violin), one or two mandolins, one or two guitars, and a double bass fiddle. Each instrument was played by a virtuoso and the original technique these men displayed was amazing. How these men, un-schooled in accepted methods of playing, could achieve such finish, such harmony, and such variety, is baffling.

There is one such band in Nashville, in which the members boast of playing together for fifteen years. Formerly there was much demand for their services, and the money thus earned in addition to what they received as gratuities from their serenading gave them a livelihood.

There is another group of instrumentalists of lower caste but no lower inspiration. These are the players who make instruments of various pieces of wood and metal they find. For instance, a wash-

44

board played with thimbles on the fingers furnishes surprisingly good percussion. A suspended piece of iron can furnish good measure pulse. Blowing into a big can sounds remarkably similar to a tuba. Occasionally one comes upon a one-stringed instrument which takes the place of the violin. It is not uncommon to find a band making use of these unorthodox instruments only, though usually one or more standard instruments are included.

Without question, the most popular instrument among Negro folk instrumentalists is the guitar. There are in Nashville, Tennessee, several clever players upon this instrument which is colloquially called a "box." Playing on this instrument is termed "pickin' the box." When a knife is used for fretting, it is called "teasing it with a knife."

The social songs can hardly be considered as rich and distinctive in melodic content as the spirituals or the blues, although the improvised accompaniment showed harmonic feeling superior to the spirituals and a development in rhythmic figures comparable only to that shown in the blues.

The melodies are not as interesting in structure and design as those of the other types of folk song. We do not find such fine melodies among them as "Deep River," and "You May Bury Me in the East," among the spirituals; or as "Little Low Mamma Blues," or "Arkansas Blues." This is due, probably, to the fact that they did not spring from deep emotional experience nor, originally, from serious attempts at description of events. Instead, they were created for dance purposes, and that fact explains the highly developed rhythm of the accompaniment. I have not found a song of this class in waltz time. All of those I have encountered have been in duple and quadruple time, slow and fast, distinguished by rhythmic figures.

The "barber shop" or "corner" quartet is quite as distinct a folk organization as the string-band. It is composed generally of members with high musical sensitiveness, with a keen aptitude for chord structure. It is stimulating to hear these men sing numbers of songs free of discords, using, frequently, chromatic harmonies in which they show a keen delight.

Favorite chords of theirs are the two-seven with a sharp, the three-seven with a sharp, the six-seven with a sharp, and a defective augmented sixth chord which is used in a sort of codetta to many of their songs. A chord progression which is peculiar to them is the progression from the two-seven chord with a sharp to the subdominant chord with a sforzando effect. The sforzando is a favorite dynamic effect with them.

These quartets sing mostly spirituals, though they do not limit themselves to them. The following is a song sung just as they sing it, including this peculiar chord progression and the cross-relations.

To collect and study these songs has been a pleasurable task. It is my fervent hope that all who sing these songs from time to time may become immersed in their pure, strong beauty.

RISE, SHINE, FOR THY LIGHT IS A-COMIN'

O 'rise! shine! for thy light is-a-comin',
'rise shine

'rise! shine! for thy light is-a- comin', O 'rise! shine! for thy
'rise shine 'rise shine

light is a- comin' My Lord says he's comin' bye'n'bye. *FINE*

LEADER   CHORUS
1. This is the year of Ju-bi-lee   My Lord says he
2.* In- tend to shout an' nev-er stop
3. Wet or dry * In- tend to try

LEADER
com-in' bye'n'bye, My Lord has set his peo-ple free
Un- til I reach the mountain-top
To serve the Lord un- til I die

CHORUS   D.S.
My Lord says he's com- in' bye 'n' bye. O

* I intend

47

GOOD MORNING EVERYBODY

RIDE ON KING JESUS

I WANT TO BE READY

50

GOD IS A GOD

God is a God! God don't nev-er change!

FINE

God is a God An' He al--ways will be God!

VERSES

1. He made the sun to shine by day, He
2. The earth his footstool an' heav'n his throne, The

made the sun to show the way, He made the stars to
whole cre-a-tion all His own, His love an' power

D.C.

show their light, He made the moon to shine by night, sayin'
will pre-vail, His pro-mis-es will nev-er fail, sayin'

SUNDAY MORNIN' BAN

ban' And none can cross but the
A ban' of an - gels
I'm pur - chased by the

sanc - ti - fied.
comin' for me.
dy - in' Lamb. Sun-day mor-nin' ban'. O

D.C.

Sun-day mor-nin' ban'.

AFTER 'WHILE

LEADER   CHORUS

1. After 'while, on!   Af - ter 'while on!
2. Pray   on!   Pray   on!
3. Shout   on!   Shout   on!

Some sweet day af - ter 'while   I'm goin' up to see my
Some sweet day af - ter 'while   Pray an' time will soon be
Some sweet day af - ter 'while   shout an' time will soon be

Je - sus, O O O   some sweet day af - ter 'while.
o - ver, O O O   some sweet day af - ter 'while.
o - ver, O O O   some sweet day af - ter 'while.

THE ROCKS AND THE MOUNTAINS

O the rocks and the mountains shall all flee a-way, And you shall have a new hid-ing place that day.

LEADER
Sinner, sinner, give up your heart to God,
Seeker, seeker, give up your heart to God,
Mourner, mourner, give up your heart to God,

CHORUS
And you shall have a new hid-ding place that day. O the

KEEP ME FROM SINKING DOWN

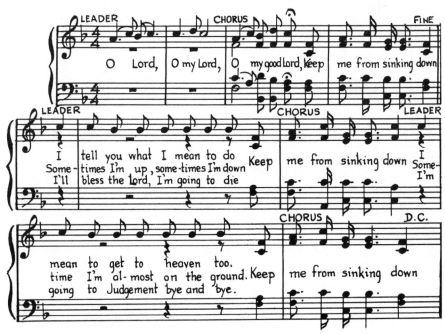

LEADER O Lord, O my Lord, CHORUS O my good lord, keep me from sinking down

LEADER
I tell you what I mean to do
Some-times I'm up, some-times I'm down
I'll bless the lord, I'm going to die

CHORUS
Keep me from sinking down

LEADER
I Some- I'm

mean to get to heaven too.
time I'm al-most on the ground. Keep
going to Judgement bye and bye.

CHORUS
me from sinking down

54

TRYIN' TO GET HOME

LEADER

1. Lord I'm bear-in' heavy bur-dens, Tryin' to get home _____
2. Lord I'm climb-in' high mountains, Tryin' to get home _____

CHORUS

_____ Lord I'm bear - in' heavy bur-dens, Try-in' to get
_____ Lord I'm climb - in' high mount-ains, Try-in' to get

home _____ Lord I'm bear - in' heavy
home Lord I'm climb - in' high

bur-dens, Lord I'm bear - in' heavy bur-dens, Lord I'm
mount-ains, Lord I'm climb - in' high mount-ains, Lord I'm

bear - in' heavy bur-dens, Try - in' to get home.
climb - in' high mount-ains, Try - in' to get home.

3. Lord, I'm standin' hard trials
   Tryin' to get home etc.

YOU MAY BURY ME IN THE EAST

1. You may bury me in the East,
2. In that dreadful Judgment day,

bury me in the West, But I'll hear the trumpet
wings and fly a-way; For to hear the trumpet

sound ___ in-a that morning.
sound ___ in-a that morning.

In-a that morning my Lord, How I long to go ___ For to hear the

trumpet sound ___ in-a that morn-ing.

3. Good old Christians, in that day
   We'll take wings and fly away
   For to hear the trumpet sound
   In-a that morning.
         Refrain.

I'LL BE THERE

SITTIN' DOWN BESIDE O' THE LAMB

3. I'll let you know befo' I go
Cho - Sittin' down beside o' the Lamb
Leader- Whether I love the Lord or no
Cho - Sittin' down beside o' the Lamb.

THE RELIGION THAT MY LORD GAVE ME

59

ROCK OF AGES

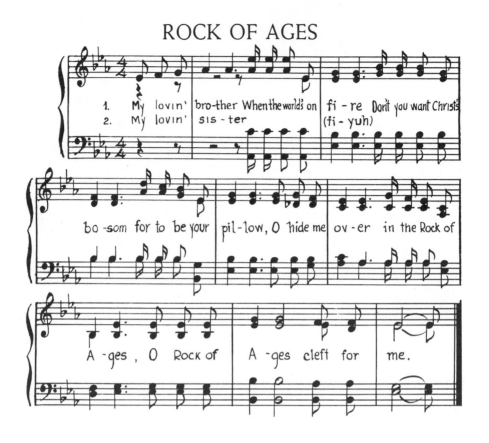

1. My lovin' bro-ther When the world's on fi-re Don't you want Christ's
2. My lovin' sis-ter (fi-yuh)

bo-som for to be your pil-low, O hide me ov-er in the Rock of

A-ges, O Rock of A-ges cleft for me.

YOU SHALL REAP

You shall reap jes what you sow, You shall reap what you sow On the

mountain, in the val-ley, You shall reap jes what you sow.

FINE

1. Brother
2. Sister
3. Sinner

THE GIFT OF GOD

O the gift of God is e - ter - nal life, e -
ter - nal life; e - ter - nal life, O the gift of God is e -
ter - nal life And the wa - ges of sin is death.

FINE

VERSES

1. When I was seek-ing Je-sus, And
2. When first I got con - ver-ted, I

thought he couldn't be found, The grace of God came
had no doubts at all, But I've had so ma - ny

D.C.

in my soul, And turned me all a - round.
crosses That I feel the least of all.

3. I wonder where's my dear mother
   She's been gone so long
   I think I hear her shouting
   Around the Throne of God.

4. Yonder comes my brother
   Whom I loved so well
   But by his disobedience
   Has made his home in hell.

61

STEADY, JESUS LISTENIN'

Stead-y Je-sus lis-ten-in'

Stead-y Jesus lis-ten-in'

Stead-y Je-sus lis-ten-in' you

must be born a - gain.

VERSES

1. Stop po' sin - ner Don't you run,
2. Light-nin' flashed an' thun - ders roll,

Jes let me tell you what the light-nin' done.
made me think a - bout my po' soul.

BYE AND BYE

O Bye and bye, bye and bye

I'm goin' to lay down my heav-y load.

LEADER
1. I know my robe's goin' to fit me well.
2. Hell is deep and dark de-spair.
3. O christ-ians can't you rise and tell.

CHORUS
I'm goin' to lay down my heav-y load

LEADER
I tried it on at the
That Je-sus hath done

Stop po' sinner and

gates of hell
don't go there
all things well

CHORUS
I'm goin' to lay down my heav-y load. O

THE LORD'S BEEN HERE

1. The Lord's been here and blessed my soul ___ The
2. I ain't goin' lay my re-li-gion down ___ I

Lord's been here and blessed my soul, O glo-ry, The
ain't goin' lay my re-li-gion down, O glo-ry, I

Lord's been here and blessed my soul ___ The
ain't goin' lay my re-li-gion down ___ I

Lord's been here and blessed my soul.
ain't goin' lay my re-li-gion down.

3. Goin' to shoulder up my heavy cross.

64

SIT DOWN SERVANT, SIT DOWN

Sit down servant, Sit down! Sit down servant, Sit down!

Sit down! Sit down!

Sit down, servant, Sit down! Sit down an' rest a little while.

Sit down! Sit down an' rest a little while.

Verse

1. know you mighty tired so sit down,
2. know you shoutin' happy so sit down,

Sit down!

Know you mighty tired so sit down!
Know you shoutin' happy so sit down!

Sit down!

* I know

AIN'T YOU GLAD YOU GOT GOOD RELIGION?

POOR ME

1. I'm some-times up, I'm sometimes down, Trouble will bur-y me
2. Hal - le - lu - jah to the Lamb, Trouble will bur-y me

down; But still my soul feels heav'nly bound Trouble will bur-y me
down; The Lord is on the giv-ing hand, Trouble will bur-y me

REFRAIN

down; O brethe-ren, Poor me, Poor me, Trou-ble will bur-y me

down. Poor me, Poor me, Trou-ble will bur-y me down.

3. Sometimes I think I'm ready to drop,
   Trouble will bury me down;
   But thank my Lord, I do not stop,
   Trouble will bury me down.
   O bretheren! - *Ref*.

SHEPHERD, SHEPHERD

Shepherd, Shepherd, where'd you lose your sheep?

Shepherd, Shepherd, where'd you lose your sheep?

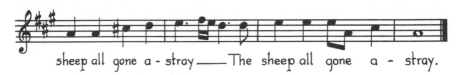

Shepherd, Shepherd, where'd you lose your sheep? O the

sheep all gone a - stray ——— The sheep all gone a - stray.

2. Shepherd, Shepherd, where'd you leave your lambs?
  "   "   "   "   "   "   "
  "   "   "   "   "   "   "
O the sheep all gone astray,
The sheep all gone astray.

3. I pray to the Lord to bring them back someday
  " " " " " " " " " "
  " " " " " " " " " "
O the sheep all gone astray,
The sheep all gone astray.

I WENT DOWN IN THE VALLEY

Solo

1. O broth-ers let's go down, let's go down, let's go down,
2. O sis-ters let's go down, let's go down, let's go down,
3. O chil-dren let's go down, let's go down, let's go down,
4. O preach-ers let's go down, let's go down, let's go down,
5. By-an'-by we'll all go down, all go down, all go down,

O broth-ers let's go down, down in the val-ley to pray. As
O sis-ters let's go down, down in the val-ley to pray. As
O chil-dren let's go down, down in the val-ley to pray. As
O preach-ers let's go down, down in the val-ley to pray. As
By-an'-by we'll all go down, down in the val-ley to pray. As

REFRAIN

I went down in the val-ley to pray, Study-ing a-bout that

good old way. O who shall wear the star-ry crown, Good

1. Lord, show me the way, As
2. Lord, show me the way.

IT'S ME

It's me it's me, O Lord, Standing in the need of pray'r;

It's me, it's me, O Lord, Standing in the need of pray'r.

Repeat pp
FINE

1. Not my brother, but it's me, O Lord, Standing in the need of pray'r;
2. Not my sis-ter, but it's me, O Lord, Standing in the need of pray'r;
3. Not my mother, but it's me, O Lord, Standing in the need of pray'r;
4. Not my el-der, but it's me, O Lord, Standing in the need of pray'r;

D.C.

Not my brother, but it's me, O Lord, Standing in the need of pray'r.
Not my sis-ter, but it's me, O Lord, Standing in the need of pray'r.
Not my mother, but it's me, O Lord, Standing in the need of pray'r.
Not my el-der, but it's me, O Lord, Standing in the need of pray'r.

I WON'T STOP PRAYING

I COULDN'T HEAR NOBODY PRAY

* The interjections used here are not the only ones which can be used, but may be changed according to the emotions of the leader.

† Let this stanza be exceedingly slow, about half as fast as the others, and the chorus very soft. But go into the refrain a tempo.

73

SHOW ME THE WAY

LEADER

O my good Lord, ___ O my good Lord, ___ O

CHORUS

Show me the way, Show me the way,

___ my good Lord, ___ En-ter the char-i-ot, trav-el a-long.   FINE

Show me the way, En-ter the char-i-ot, trav-el a-long.

LEADER

1.
2. Going to serve my Lord while I have breath,
3. When I get to Heav'n and get on my shoes,

No-ah sent out a mourn-ing dove,

CHORUS   LEADER

En-ter the char-i-ot, tra-vel; a-long; Which brought back a
En-ter the char-i-ot, tra-vel a-long; So I can
En-ter the char-i-ot, tra-vel a-long; Going to fly about Heav'n

                                    CHORUS   D.C.

tok-en of a heav-en-ly love, En-ter the char-i-ot, trav-el a-long.
see Him aft-er death, En-ter the char-i-ot, trav-el a-long.
and tell the news En-ter the char-i-ot, trav-el a-long.

LEAD ME TO THE ROCK

Lead me, Lead me, my Lord; Lead me, Lead me to the Rock that is

high-er than I. O,

I. 1. The man who loves to serve the Lord,
2. As I go down the stream of time,
3. Ole Sa-tan's mad and I am glad,

Lead me to the Rock that is high-er than I_ Will sure-ly get his
Lead me to the Rock that is high-er than I_ I leave this sin-ful
Lead me to the Rock that is high-er than I_ He missed that soul he

D.C.

just re-ward, Lead me to the rock that is high-er than I. O,
world be-hind, Lead me to the rock that is high-er than I. O,
thought he had, Lead me to the rock that is high-er than I. O,

LORD I WANT TO BE A CHRISTIAN

1. Lord, I want to be a Chris-tian In a my heart, in a my
2. Lord, I want to be more lov-ing In a my heart, in a my
3. Lord, I want to be more ho-ly In a my heart, in a my
4. I don't want to be like Ju-das In a my heart, in a my
5 Lord, I want to be like Je-sus In a my heart, in a my

heart, Lord, I want to be a Chris-tian In a my heart.
heart, Lord, I want to be more lov-ing In a my heart.
heart, Lord, I want to be more ho-ly In a my heart.
heart, I don't want to be like Ju-das In a my heart.
heart, Lord, I want to be like Je-sus In a my heart.

REFRAIN

In a my heart _____ In a my heart, _____
In a my heart, In a my heart,

Lord, I want to be a Chris-tian In a my heart.

STEAL AWAY AND PRAY

A LITTLE TALK WITH JESUS

O a lit-tle talk with Je-sus makes it right, all right, Lit-tle talk with

Je-sus makes it right, all right, Troubles of ev-'ry kind,

FINE

Thank God I'll al-ways find That a lit-tle talk with Je-sus makes it right.

My broth - er, I re-mem-ber when I was a sin-ner lost, I
Some - times the fork-ed lightning and mut-ter-ing thun-der, too, Of
My broth - er and my sis-ter, you have tri - als here like me, When

cried, "Have mer - cy, Je - sus," But still my soul wass tossed,
tri - als and temp-ta - tions Make it hard for me and you,
we are try-ing to serve the Lord, And win the vic-to - ry,

Till I heard King Jesus say, "Come here, I am the way;"
But Jesus is our friend, He'll keep us to the end;
Old Sa-tan fights us hard Our journ-ey to re-tard;

D.C.

And a lit-tle talk with Jesus makes it right.
And a lit-tle talk with Jesus makes it right.
But a lit-tle talk with Jesus makes it right.

A LITTLE TALK WITH JESUS
(SECOND VERSION)

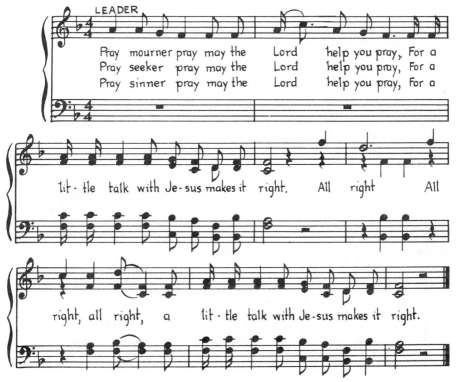

LEADER

Pray mourner pray may the Lord help you pray, For a
Pray seeker pray may the Lord help you pray, For a
Pray sinner pray may the Lord help you pray, For a

lit-tle talk with Je-sus makes it right. All right All

right, all right, a lit-tle talk with Je-sus makes it right.

GIVE ME JESUS

1. I heard my mother say, I heard my mother say, I
2. † Dark mid-night, was my cry, Dark mid-night, was my cry, Dark
3. In the morn-ing when I rise, In the morn-ing when I rise, In the
4. And when I come to die, And when I come to die, And

REFRAIN

heard my mother say, "Give me Je - sus."
midnight, was my cry, "Give me Je - sus."
morning when I rise, Give me Je - sus. Give me Je-sus, Give me
when I come to die, Give me Je - sus.

Je - sus; You may have all this world, Give me Je - sus.

† *I.e.* At dark midnight.

ROLL ON

Roll on, roll on, sweet moments roll on, And let these poor

FINE

pil-grims go home, go home.
1. When I was blind and
2. The Heav'n-ly land so

D.C.

could not see, King Je - sus brought that light to me.
bright and fair, There are ver-y few seem go - ing there.

PRAY ON

LEADER

1. In the river of Jor-dan John baptized,
2. We bap-tize all that come by faith,
3. Here's an-other one come to be bap-tized,

CHORUS

How I long to be bap-tized, In the river of Jor-dan
How I long to be bap-tized, We bap-tize all that
How I long to be bap-tized, Here's an-other one come to

John bap-tized un - to the dy - ing Lamb.
come by faith un - to the dy - ing Lamb.
be bap-tized un - to the dy - ing Lamb.

Pray on! Pray on! Pray on! you mourn-ing souls

Pray on! Pray on un - to the dy-ing Lamb.

DO LORD REMEMBER ME

1. Do Lord, do Lord, Do re-mem-ber me,
2. When I'm in trou-ble, Do re-mem-ber me,

Do Lord, do Lord, Do re-mem-ber me,
When I'm in trou-ble, Do re-mem-ber me.

Do Lord, do Lord, Do re-mem-ber me, O
When I'm in trou-ble, Do re-mem-ber me, O

Do Lord re - mem - ber me.
Do Lord re - mem - ber me.

3. When I'm dyin'
   Do remember me.

4. When this world's on fire,
   Do remember me.

82

LORD MAKE ME MORE HOLY

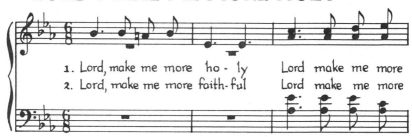

3. Lord, make me more humble, etc.

4. Lord, make me more righteous, etc.

IN THIS LAN'

1. Lord help the po' and the need-y, In this lan'
2. Lord help the wi-dows and the orphans, In this lan'

In this lan', Lord help the po' and the need-y, In this
In this lan', Lord help the widows and the or-phans, In this

lan', In this lan', In that great getting up
lan', In this lan', In that great getting up

morn-ing we shall face an-oth-er sun, Lord
morn-ing we shall face an-oth-er sun, Lord

help the po' and the need-y, In this lan' In this lan.
help the widows and the or-phans, In this lan' In this lan'.

* Flatted third.

3. Lord help the motherless children, etc.

4. Lord help the hypocrite members, etc.

5. Lord help the long tongue liars, etc.

COME HERE LORD

Come here, Lord! come here, Lord! come here, Lord!

Sin- ners, cry-ing, "Come here Lord!" Lord!" O, lit-tle did I think He

was so nigh, Sin- ners cry-ing, "Come here, Lord!" He

spoke, and He made me laugh and cry, Sin- ners cry-ing, "Come here, Lord!"

2. O mourners, if you will believe,
The grace of God you will recieve.

3. Some seek God's face, but don't seek right,
Pray a little by day and none at night.

4. O sinner, now you had better pray,
For Satan's 'round you ev'ry day.

BE WITH ME

1. Be with me Lord! Be with me! _____
2. When I'm in trou-ble, Be with me! _____
3. When I'm dy-ing, Be with me! _____

_____ Be with me Lord! Be with me! _____
_____ When I'm in troub-le, Be with me! _____
_____ When I'm dy-ing, Be with me! _____

When I'm on my lone-some jour-ney,

I want Je - - sus Be with me.

COME HERE JESUS IF YOU PLEASE

LEADER   CHORUS

1. No harm have I done you on my knees. No
2. O Lord have mercy on po' me. O

harm have I done you on my knees. When you see me on my
Lord have mercy on po' me.

knees _____ Come here Je-sus if you please.

O MAKE ME HOLY

O make-a-me ho — ho — ly

I do love, I do love, O make-a-me

ho — ho-ly I do love the Lord

FINE

LEADER

Did you ev - er see such love be - fore,
I'm born of God I know I am,
Down on my knees when the light passed by,

CHORUS

I do love, I do love, King Je - sus preaching
I'm purchased by the
I thought my soul would

LEADER

CHORUS

to the poor, I do love the Lord. O make-a-me
dy - ing Lamb,
rise and fly,

LEADER

D.S.

87

COME DOWN

Come down, ... Come down, my Lord! Come down,

Way down in Egypt land. 1. Jesus Christ, He died for me, ... Way down in Egypt land;

Je- sus Christ, He set me free, Way down in E- gypt land.

2. Born of God I know I am,
   Way down in Egypt land;
   I'm purchased by the dying Lamb,
   Way down in Egypt land.
   Come down, etc.

3. Peter walked upon the sea,
   Way down in Egypt land;
   And Jesus told him, "Come to Me,"
   Way down in Egypt land.
   Come down, etc.

DON'T YOU LET NOBODY TURN YOU ROUN'

Don't you let no-bo-dy turn you 'roun', turn you 'roun' turn you 'roun' Don't you let no-bo-dy turn you 'roun', keep the straight an' the nar-row way.

Verses

1. 'T was at the river of Jor-dan, Bap-tism was be-gun, John bap-tized the mul-ti-tude, But he sprinkled na-ry one;

2. The baptis' they go by wa-ter, The methodes' go by lan', But when they get to hea-ven They'll shake each oth-er's han'.

3. — You may be a good baptis'
An' a good methodes' as well,
But if you aint the pure in heart
Yo' soul is boun' for hell.

YO' LOW DOWN WAYS

Yo' low-down ways, yo' low-down ways, God's goin' to get you 'bout yo'
low-down ways, yo' low-down ways, yo' low-down ways,

God's goin' to get you 'bout yo' low down ways.

VERSES LEADER
1. You talk a-bout yo' el-der when he's tryin' to preach the word,
2. You talk a-bout yo' neighbor when he's tryin' to praise the Lord.
3. You talk a-bout yo' sis-ter when she's on her knees a-prayin'

CHORUS   LEADER
God's goin' to get you 'bout yo' low-down ways, You talk a-bout yo' el-der when he's
                                               You talk a-bout yo' neighbor when he's
                                               You talk a-bout yo' sister when she's

tryin' to preach the word,
tryin' to praise the Lord, God's goin' to get you 'bout yo' low-down ways.
on her knees a-prayin'

THANK GOD I'M ON MY WAY TO HEAVEN

VERSES
1. You may talk a-bout me jes as much as you please, You may
2. I met my sis-ter the o-ther day, I

spread my name a-broad, But ev-er-y lie that you
asked her "how do you do"? She says I'm doing mighty well an' I

tell on me jes Throws me higher in the heav'n,
thank God too, Thank God! I'm on my way to heav'n,

REFRAIN
Heav'n, heav'n, Thank God! I'm on my way to heav'n.

GOT TO GO TO JUDGMENT

MY LORD WHAT A MOURNING

YOU'D BETTER RUN

WHEN THE TRAIN COMES ALONG

When the train comes a-long, when the train comes a-long, I'll

meet you at the station when the train comes a-long. When the train comes along.

LEADER

1. I may be blind an' can-not see, But I'll
2. I may be lame an' can-not walk, But I'll

meet you at the station when the train comes a-long. When the

WISH I'S IN HEAVEN SETTIN' DOWN

1. Wish I's in heaven settin' down, settin' down
2. Wouldn't get tired no mo', tired no mo'

wish I's in heaven settin' down settin' down
wouldn't get tired no mo' Tired no mo'

O Ma- ry, O Mar- tha

wish I's in heaven settin' down.
wouldn't get tired no mo'.

2. Wouldn't have nothin' to do
3. Try on my long white robe
4. Sit at my Jesus' feet

OPEN THE WINDOW NOAH

I'M WORKIN ON THE BUILDIN'

I'M GOING BACK WITH JESUS

*3. And He's going to bring my mother with Him When He comes

* In the third Verse the singer must add a beat to fit the words "And He's."

THIS OL' TIME RELIGION

HAMMERING

'TWAS ON ONE SUNDAY MORNING

1. Twas on one Sun-day morn-ing, Sunday morn-ing, Sun-day morn-ing— Twas on one Sun-day morn-ing, Just 'bout the break of day.

2. An Angel came down from Heaven
Came down from Heaven, came down from Heaven.
An Angel came down from Heaven,
And rolled the stone away.

3. John and Peter came running,
Came a-running, came a-running
John and Peter came running,
And found an empty tomb.

4. Mary and Martha came weeping
Came a-weeping, came a-weeping
Mary and Martha came weeping
And lo! their Lord had gone.

THEY LED MY LORD AWAY

They led my Lord a-way, a-way, a-way; They
led my Lord a-way, O tell me where to find Him find Him.

1. The Jews and Romans, in-a one band,   Tell me where to find Him,
2. They led Him up to Pi-late's bar,   Tell me where to find Him,
3. Old Pilate said, "I wash my hands,"   Tell me where to find Him,

They cru-ci-fied the Son of Man,   Tell me where to find Him.
But the Jews could not condemn Him there,   Tell me where to find Him.
"I find no fault in this just Man,"   Tell me where to find Him.

HE NEVER SAID A MUMBLIN' WORD

1. They led Him to Pilate's bar,
2. They all cried "Crucify Him," Not a
3. They nailed Him to the tree,

word, not a word, not a word, not a word. They all cried "Crucify
They nailed Him to the

bar,
Him," Not a word, not a word, not a word, not a word, They
tree,

led Him to Pilate's bar,
all cried "Crucify Him," But he never said a mumblin'
nailed Him to the tree,

word, Not a word, not a word, not a word, not a word.

4. They pierced Him in the side,
5. He hung his head and died,
6. They laid Him in the tomb,
7. Wasn't that a pity and a shame.

CALVARY

Very slowly

Cal-va-ry, — Cal-va-ry, Cal-va-ry —

Cal-va-ry Cal-va-ry, — Cal-va-ry, Sure-ly He

FINE

died on — Cal-va-ry — Ev-'ry time I — think a-bout

Je-sus, Ev-'ry time I — think a-bout Je-sus, Ev-'ry time I

D.C.

think a-bout Je-sus, — Sure-ly He died on — Cal-va-ry.

2. Sinner, do you love my Jesus ?
   Surely He died on Calvary.
   Calvary, Calvary, etc.

3. We are climbing Jacob's ladder,
   Surely He died on Calvary.
   Calvary, Calvary, etc.

4. Every round goes higher and higher,
   Surely He died on Calvary.
   Calvary, Calvary, etc.

WERE YOU THERE?

1. Were you there when they cru-ci-fied my Lord? (were you
2. Were you there when they nailed Him to the tree? (to the
3. Were you there when they pierced Him in the side? (in the
4. Were you there when the sun re-fused to shine? (were you
5. Were you there when they laid Him in the tomb? (in the

there?) Were you there when they cru-ci-fied my Lord? Oh!..........
tree?) Were you there when they nailed Him to the tree? Oh!..........
side?) Were you there when they pierced Him in the side? Oh!..........
there?) Were you there when the sun re-fused to shine? Oh!..........
tomb?) Were you there when they laid Him in the tomb? Oh!..........

Sometimes it causes me to tremble, tremble, tremble, Were you
Sometimes it causes me to tremble, tremble, tremble, Were you
Sometimes it causes me to tremble, tremble, tremble, Were you
Sometimes it causes me to tremble, tremble, tremble, Were you
Sometimes it causes me to tremble, tremble, tremble, Were you

there when they cru- ci- fied my Lord?
there when they nailed Him to the tree?
there when they pierced Him in the side?
there when the sun re- fused to shine?
there when they laid Him in the tomb?

HOLY BIBLE

Very slowly

1. Ho-ly Bi - ble, Ho - ly Bi - ble,
2. O what weep-ing, O what weep-ing,
3. Weep-ing Ma - ry, weep-ing Ma-ry,
4. Doubt-ing Thom-as, doubt-ing Thom-as,
5. Great Je - ho - vah, Great Je - ho-vah,

Ho - ly Bi-ble, book di - vine, book di - vine _____
O what weep-ing o - ver me, o - ver me _____
Weep-ing Ma - ry, weep no more, weep no more _____
Doubt-ing Thom-as, doubt no more, doubt no more _____
Great Je - ho - vah, o - ver all, o - ver all _____

Be - fore I'd be a slave, I'd be bur-ied in my grave,

And go home to my Fa-ther and be saved.

106

DEATH'S GOIN' TO LAY HIS HAND ON ME

1. O sin-ner, sin-ner, you bet-ter pray, Death's goin' to lay his
2. And if you get there be-fore I do, Death's goin' to lay his
3 Some peo-ple think I have no grace, Death's goin' to lay his

cold i - cy hands on me, Or your sou'll get lost at the
cold i - cy hands on me, Tell all my friends I'm a-
cold i - cy hands on me, But I'll see Je - sus —

judg-ment-day, Death's goin' to lay his cold i - cy hands on me.
com-ing too, Death's goin' to lay his cold i - cy hands on me.
face to face, Death's goin' to lay his cold i - cy hands on me.

REFRAIN

Cry-ing, "O — Lord!" cry-ing, "O my Lord!" Cry-ing, "O —

slower and slower

Lord!" Death's goin' to lay his cold i - cy hands on me.

I MUST WALK MY LONESOME VALLEY

1. I must walk my lone-some val - ley, I got to walk it for my-self, No-bo-dy else can walk it for me, I got to walk it for my - self.
2. I must go and stand my tri - al, I got to stand it for my-self, No-bo-dy else can stand it for me, I got to stand it for my - self.
3. Je - sus walked his lone-some val - ley, He had to walk it for him-self, No-bo-dy else could walk it for him, He had to walk it for him - self.

WE SHALL WALK THROUGH THE VALLEY

1. We shall walk through the valley and the shadow of death, We shall walk through the val - ley in peace, If Je - sus Him-self shall be our lea - - der We shall walk through the val - ley in peace.
2. We shall meet our bro - ther there ___ We shall meet our bro - ther there,
3. There will be no weep - ing there ___ There will be no weep - ing there,

SOON A WILL BE DONE

Soon-a will be done with the trouble of this world,

Soon-a will be done with the trouble of this world.

Soon-a will be done with this trouble of this world

Going to live with God____.

2. Come my brother and go with me
   Come my brother and go with me
   Come my brother and go with me
   Let King Jesus make you free.

3. When I get to heav'n I will sing and tell
   When I get to heav'n I will sing and tell
   When I get to heav'n I will sing and tell
   How I did shun both death and hell.

SOON A WILL BE DONE
(SECOND VERSION)

Soon-a will be done-a with the troubles of the world, Troubles of the world, ____The trou-bles of the world. Soon-a will be done-a with the trou-bles of the world. Goin' home to live with God.

FINE

1. No more weeping and a-wail-ing, No more weep-ing and a wail-ing,
2. I want t' meet my mother, I want t' meet my mother,
3. I want t' meet my Je-sus, I want t' meet my Je-sus,

No more weeping and a-wail-ing, I'm goin' to live with God.
I want t' meet my moth-er, I'm goin' to live with God.
I want t' meet my Je-sus, I'm goin' to live with God.

D.C.

LISTEN TO THE LAMBS

JESUS GOIN' TO MAKE UP MY DYING BED

CHORUS

You needn't min' my dy - in', you needn't min' my dy - in',

FINE

You needn't min' my dy - in', Je-sus goin' to make up my dy-in' bed.

LEADER

1. In my dy-in' room I know, some-body's goin' to cry,

All I ask you to do for me, jes close my dy - in' eyes.

CHORUS

I'll be sleepin' in Je - sus, I'll be sleepin' in Je-sus

I'll be sleepin' in Je - sus, Je-sus goin' to make up my dy-in' bed.

LEADER

2. In my dy-in' room I know, somebody's goin' to mourn,

All I ask you to do for me jes give that bell a tone.

CHORUS

I'll be rest-in' eas-y, I'll be rest-in' eas-y,

I'll be rest-in' eas-y, Je-sus goin' to make up my dy-in' bed.

LEADER

When I get to heav v'n I want you to be there too,

When I cry out "ho-ly" I want you to say so too.

DEATH AIN'T NOTHIN' BUT A ROBBER

YOU HEAR THE LAMBS A-CRYING

You hear the lambs a - cry-in,'

Hear the lambs a - cry - in,' Hear the lambs a-

1.

cry - in,' O Shep-herd feed my sheep. You

D.S. 2. FINE

feed my sheep.

LEADER

1. My Sa - viour spoke these words so sweet,
2. Lord I love Thee Thou dost know
3. Was - n't that an aw - ful shame

sayin' " Peter if you love me
O give me grace to
He hung three hours in

CHORUS

O Shep-herd feed my sheep

feed my sheep."
love Thee more."
mor-tal pain.

D.S.

Shep - herd feed my Sheep. You

114

O WRETCHED MAN

1. O wretched man that I am
2. I'm bowed down with a burden of woe

O wretched man that I am
I'm bowed down with a burden of woe

O wretched man that I am
I'm bowed down with a burden of woe

am, O who will de - liv - er po' me.
woe, O who will de - liv - er po' me.

DOWN ON ME

Down on me _____ Down on me _____

Looks like ev'ry - body in the whole round world's down on me.

Talk a - bout me, much as you please I'll talk a-bout you when I get on my knees
Sometimes I'm up, sometimes I'm down, Sometimes I'm al - most on the ground
Heaven's so high, I am so low, Don't know if I'll ever get to heaven or no

Looks like ev - 'ry - body in the whole round world's down on me.

115

THE HAMMERS KEEP RINGING

1. The hammers keep ring-ing ___ on some-body's cof-fin ___ The hammers keep ring-ing ___ on somebod dy's cof-fin ___ The hammers keep ring-ing ___ on some-bo-dy's cof-fin ___ Makes me know my time ain't long.

2. The hearse wheels rol-ling ___ somebody to the grave-yard ___ The hearse wheels rol-ling ___ some-bo-dy to the grave-yard ___ The hearse wheels rol-ling ___ some-bo-dy to the grave-yard ___ Makes me know my time ain't long.

3. Tell that po' sinner, he'd better get religion
   Tell that po' sinner, he'd better get religion
   Tell that po' sinner, he'd better get religion
   For I know his time ain't long.

THE ANGELS DONE BOWED DOWN

1. While Jesus was a-hanging upon the cross, the angels kept quiet till God went off, And the angels hung their harps on the willow trees to give satisfaction till God was pleased.

2. His soul went up on the pillar of cloud, O God he moved and the heavens did bow, Jehovah's sword was at his side, On the empty air He began to ride.

3. "Go down angels to the flood
Blow out the sun, turn the moon into blood!
Come back angels bolt the door
The time thats been will be no more!"

WHERE SHALL I GO?

* An idiomatic expression.

WHEN I'M DEAD

When I'm dead don't you grieve aft-er me, When I'm
dead don't you grieve aft-er me, When I'm dead don't you
grieve aft-er me, By and by don't you grieve aft-er me.

1. Pale Horse and Rider have taken my mother a-way, Pale Horse and Rider have
2. Pale Horse and Rider____ stop at ev-er-y door, Pale Horse and Rider
3. Cold i-cy hand____ took my father a-way, Cold i-cy hand____

taken my mother a-way, Pale Horse and Rid-er have
stop at ev-e-ry door, Pale Horse and Rid-er____
took my father a-way, Cold i-cy hand____

taken my mother a-way, By and by don't you grieve aft-er me.
stop at ev-e-ry door, By and by don't you grieve aft-er me.
took my father a-way, By and by don't you grieve aft-er me.

O MOTHER DON'T YOU WEEP

gone gone gone

When I'm gone, when I'm gone, when I'm gone, gone, gone, when I'm
mother, don't you weep when I am gone.

FINE

For I'm goin' to Heav'n a-bove, Go-ing
O____ mother meet me there, mother

to the God I love, O____ mother, don't you weep when I am gone.
meet me in the air, O____ moth-er, don't you weep when I am gone.

D.C.

119

DANIEL SAW THE STONE

Dan - iel saw the stone, Roll - ing___ roll - ing,

FINE

Dan - iel saw the stone Cut out the mountain with-out hands.

1. Nev - er saw such a man be - fore, Cut out the mountain without hands.
2. Dan - iel pray'd in the li - ons' den, Cut out the mountain without hands.
3. Dan - iel pray'd three times a day, Cut out the mountain without hands.

D.C.

Preaching gos-pel to the poor, Cut out the mountain without hands.
Spite of all those wick-ed men, Cut out the mountain without hands.
Drive the dev - il far a - way, Cut out the mountain without hands.

DANIEL SAW THE STONE
(SECOND VERSION)

LEADER

1. Dan-iel saw the stone, ____
2. Have you seen that stone? Hewn out the mountain,

CHORUS

Dan-iel saw the stone ____ O

Have you seen that stone? Hewn out the mountain,

Dan-iel saw the stone, ____

Have you seen that stone? Hewn out the mountain,

Tear-ing down the king-dom of this world.

3. Yes, I saw that stone, etc:

4. You'd better seek that stone, etc:

5. Jesus was the stone, etc:

6. Going to preach about that stone, etc:

7. O, that holy stone.

121

JESUS IS RISEN FROM THE DEAD

LEADER

In - a this-a band we have sweet mu - sic,

In - a this-a band we have sweet mu - sic, In - a this-a band we

have sweet mu - sic, Je - sus is ris - en from the dead.

FINE

Verse

Go, tell Ma-ry and Mar-tha, Go and tell Ma-ry and Mar-tha,
Go, tell John and Pe-ter, Go and tell John and Pe-ter,
Go, tell doubt-ing Thom-as, Go and tell doubt-ing Thomas,
Go, tell Paul and Si-las, Go and tell Paul and Si-las,
Go, tell all th' A-pos-tles, Go and tell all th' A-pos-tles,
Go, tell ev - 'ry-bod-y, Go and tell ev - 'ry-bod-y,

Go and tell Ma-ry and Martha, "Yes, Je-sus is ris-en from the dead."
Go and tell John and Peter, "Yes, Je-sus is ris-en from the dead."
Go and tell doubt - ing Thomas, "Yes, Je-sus is ris-en from the dead."
Go and tell Paul and Si-las, "Yes, Je-sus is ris-en from the dead."
Go and tell all th' Apos-tles, "Yes, Je-sus is ris-en from the dead."
Go and tell ev - 'ry-bod-y, "Yes, Je-sus is ris-en from the dead."

STEAL AWAY TO JESUS

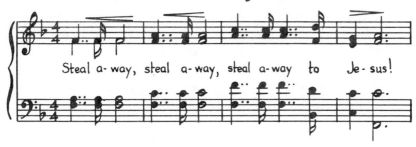

Steal a-way, steal a-way, steal a-way to Je-sus!

Steal a-way, steal a-way home, I ain't got long to stay here!

My Lord calls me, He calls me by the thun-der;
Green trees are bend-ing, Poor sin - ner stands a - trem-bling;
Tomb stones are burst-ing, Poor sin - ner stands a - trem-bling;
My Lord calls me, He calls me by the light-ning,

(die away)

The trum-pet sounds with in- a my soul, I ain't got long to stay here.

123

LITTLE DAVID

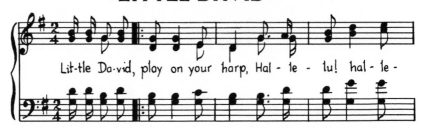

Lit-tle Da-vid, play on your harp, Hal - le - lu! hal - le -

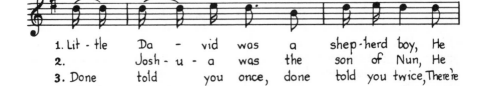

lu! Lit-tle Da-vid play on your harp, Hal - le - lu! Lit - tle Dav-vid   lu!

1. Lit - tle   Da – vid   was   a   shep - herd boy, He
2.   Josh - u - a   was   the   son   of Nun, He
3. Done   told   you once, done   told you twice, There're

killed Go - li - ath and   shout - ed for   joy.
nev - er would quit   till the   work   was   done.
sin - ners in hell   for   shoot - ing dice.

INCHING ALONG

Keep a- inch-ing a-long, Keep a- inch-ing a-long, Je-sus will come by and -by. Keep a- inch-ing a-long, like a poor inch-worm, Je-sus will come by-and-by.

FINE

1. It was inch by inch that I sought the Lord,
2. We'll inch and inch and inch a- long,
3. O trials and trou-bles on the way,

Je-sus will come by-and-by, It was inch by inch that He
Je-sus will come by-and-by, And inch by inch till
Je-sus will come by-and-by, But we must watch as

saved my soul, Je-sus will come by-and-by. Keep a-
we get home, Je-sus will come by-and-by. Keep a-
well as pray, Je-sus will come by-and-by. Keep a-

D.S.

* The melody of this song composed of only three tones.

125

O ROCKS DON'T FALL ON ME

O rocks, don't fall on me, O rocks, don't fall on me,

FINE

O rocks, don't fall on me, Rocks and mountains, don't fall on me.

1. Look o - - - ver yon-der on Jer - ri - cho's wall,
2. In - a that great, great judg - ment day,
3. When ev - er - y star re - fus-es to shine,
4. The trump shall sound, and the dead shall rise,

Rocks and mountains, don't fall on me; And see those sin - ners
Rocks and mountains, don't fall on me; The sin - ners will run to the
Rocks and mountains, don't fall on me; I know King Je - sus
Rocks and mountains, don't fall on me; And go to man - sions

D.C.

tremble and fall, "Rocks and mount-ains, don't fall on me.
rocks and say: "Rocks and mount-ains, don't fall on me.
will-a be mine, Rocks and mount-ains, don't fall on me.
in-a the skies, Rocks and mount-ains, don't fall on me.

BEFORE THIS TIME ANOTHER YEAR

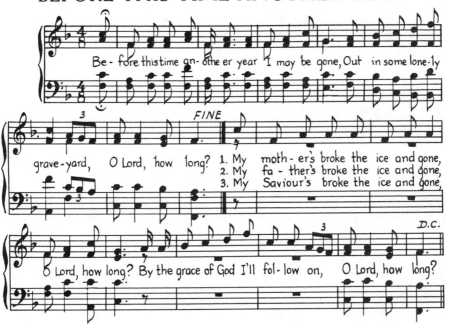

Be - fore this time an - oth er year I may be gone, Out in some lone - ly grave - yard, O Lord, how long?

FINE

1. My moth - er's broke the ice and gone,
2. My fa - ther's broke the ice and gone,
3. My Saviour's broke the ice and gone,

O Lord, how long? By the grace of God I'll fol - low on, O Lord, how long?

D.C.

SOMEBODY'S BURIED IN THE GRAVEYARD

Somebody's bur-ied in the graveyard, Some-bod - y's bur-ied in the sea,

Going to get up in the morning a shouting, Going to join Ju - bi - lee.

FINE

1. Al - though you see me com - ing a - long so,
2. I have some friends be - fore me gone,
3. Some - times I'm up, some - times I'm down,

To the prom - ised land I'm bound to go.
By the grace of God I'll fol - low on.
But still my soul is heaven - ly bound.

D.C.

* *Death held a very prominent place in the mind and songs of the slave. In exact proportion to his hardships, did he sing of death and the glories of Heaven where he should receive just those things that were denied him. Heaven was to him above all else a place of rest and of shouting and jubilation.*

127

BALM IN GILEAD

There is a Balm in Gil-e-ad, To make the wounded whole, There is a

Balm in Gil-e-ad, To heal the sin-sick soul, There is a soul.

1. Some-times I feel dis-cour-aged, And think my work's in vain, But
2. Don't ev-er feel dis-cour-aged, For Je-sus is your friend, And
3. If you can-not preach like Pe-ter, If you can-not pray like Paul, You can

then the Ho-ly Spir-it Re-vives my soul a-gain. There is a
if you lack for knowledge, He'll ne'er re-fuse to lend. There is a
tell the love of Je-sus, And say, "He died for all." There is a

SING A HO THAT I HAD THE WINGS OF A DOVE

Refrain

Sing a ho that I had the wings of a dove, Sing a
ho that I had the wings of a dove. Sing a
ho that I had the wings of a dove; I'd fly a-way and be at rest.

FINE

1. Vir-gin Ma-ry had one son, I'd fly a-way and be at rest, The
2. Zion's daughters wept and mourned, I'd fly a-way and be at rest, —
3. Sin-ner man, see what a shame, I'd fly a-way and be at rest; —

D.C.

Jews and the Romans had him hung, I'd fly a-way and be at rest.
When their dy-ing Saviour groaned, I'd fly a-way and be at rest.
To trample down your Saviour's name, I'd fly a-way and be at rest.

When the preacher has worked his auditors up to a high degree of excitement, he will
often break off and extemporize some song, with his text as its basis, in which the
audience joins, and at the end of it will go on "exhorting" again. This song, which is
one of the most beautiful of our collection, was composed in this way in Robertson
County, Tennessee. It seemed at first crude and unavailable, but as it was sung
over and over again gradually reached its present musical form.

129

GOT RELIGION ALL AROUND THE WORLD

1. Christians, hold up your heads! Christians, hold up your heads! Christians,
2. Neighbor, you bear your load! Neighbor, you bear your load! Neighbor,
3. Sister, you stand the storm! Sis-ter, you stand the storm! Sis-ter,

hold up your heads!
you bear your load!
you stand the storm! Got re - li -gion all round the world, O, then I'll shout a "Glo-ry!" O,

then I'll shout a "Glo-ry!" Lord, Then I'll shout a "Glo-ry!" Got re-

li-gion all round the world, O, -li - gion all round the world.

130

MY SOUL'S BEEN ANCHORED IN THE LORD

Ain't you glad

O, my soul's been an-chored in the Lord, My

Can't you sing it!

soul's been an-chored in the Lord, My soul's been anchored in the

Tell it chil-dren!

Lord, My soul's been an-chored in the Lord.

1. Where've you been, poor sin - - - ner? O,
2. You may talk a-bout me just as much as you please, You may
3. See my fa-ther in the gos - - - pel Come

where've you been so long? Been working out of the sight of man, And my
spread my name a-broad; I'll pray for you when I get on my knees, For my
† wagging up the hill so slow, He's cry-ing now as he cried be-fore, My

Exclamations for Verses

1. O, I'm happy!	2. You can't hurt me!	3. Left my burden!
Found my Jesus!	For I'm sheltered!	At the river!
On my knees!	In my Jesus!	In the valley!

† I.e., toiling, moving slowly.

MY GOOD LORD'S DONE BEEN HERE

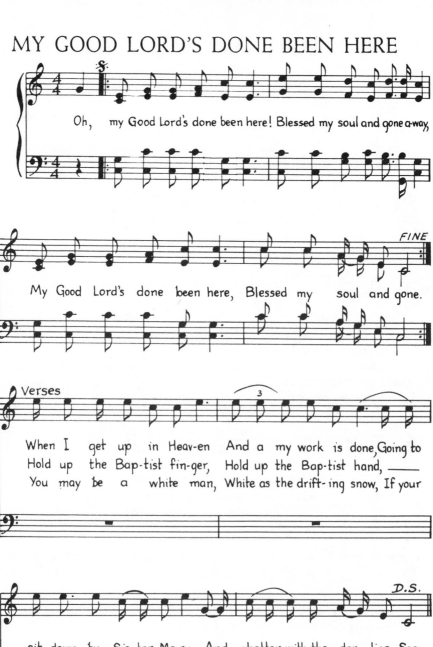

Oh, my Good Lord's done been here! Blessed my soul and gone a-way

My Good Lord's done been here, Blessed my soul and gone.

Verses

When I get up in Heav-en And a my work is done, Going to
Hold up the Bap-tist fin-ger, Hold up the Bap-tist hand, _____
You may be a white man, White as the drift-ing snow, If your

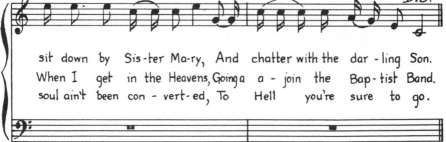

sit down by Sis-ter Ma-ry, And chatter with the dar-ling Son.
When I get in the Heavens, Going a a - join the Bap-tist Band.
soul ain't been con - vert-ed, To Hell you're sure to go.

MY SOUL'S BEEN ANCHORED IN THE LORD
(SECOND VERSION)

In the Lord, in the Lord, My soul's been anchored in the Lord.

My soul's been anchored in the Lord.

1. I'm born of God I know I am
2. Goin' shout an' pray an' nev-er stop

My soul's been anchored in the

Been purchased by the dy-in' Lamb
Un-til I reach the mountain top

Lord _____ My soul's been anchored in the

O Lord!   O Lord!___

Lord, My soul's been anchored in the Lord, My soul's been anchored in the Lord.

AT THE BAR OF GOD

I FEEL LIKE MY TIME AIN'T LONG

I feel like, I feel like, I feel like my time ain't long, I feel like, I feel like, I feel like my time ain't long.

FINE

1. Went to the graveyard the oth-er day, I feel like my time ain't long, I look'd at the place where my moth-er lay, I feel like my time ain't long.
2. Some-times I'm up—some-times I'm down, I feel like my time ain't long, And some-times I'm al-most on the ground, I feel like my time ain't long.
3. Mind out, my brother how you walk on the cross, I feel like my time ain't long, Your foot might slip and your soul get lost, I feel like my time ain't long.

THIS IS A SIN-TRYING WORLD

O, this is a sin-try-ing world   This is a sin-try-ing word   This is a sin-try-ing world,   This is a sin-try-ing world.

Leader: O, Lord!
Chorus
Help me Je-sus!
Sing it chil-dren!

1. O Heav'n is so high, and I am so low,
2. _____ Jor - dan's stream is chil-ly and wide,
3. _____ Way o - ver yonder in the harv - est fields,
4. You may bu-ry me in the East, you may bu-ry me in the West,

I don't know whether I'll ev-er get to Heav'n or no ___
None can ___ cross but the sanc - ti - fied ___
The an - gels ___ shoving at the char-i - ot wheels ___
But in that ___ morning my soul will be at rest ___

Exclamations for Verses

1. High Heaven!   2. Cold Jordan!   3. O the harvest!   4. In the Heavens!
   Hard trials!   Deep and wide!   Few laborers!   With my mother!
   Crown of Life!   Can't you cross it?   Won't you join them?   And my Saviour!

136

MY NAME'S WRITTEN ON HIGH

Hail! Hail! I be-long to the bloodwashed army, Hail! Hail!

LEADER—O well a-then!

My name's written on high.

My name's written on high

hal-le-lu-jah to the lamb! My name's written on high; King
you get there be-fore I do, My name's written on high; Look
get back, Sa-tan, let me by, My name's written on high; Going to
Go back, all the powers of hell, My name's written on high; ——
Shout, my sis-ter, you are free, My name's written on high; ——

LEADER —O well-a-then.

Je-sus died for ev-'ry man, My name's written on high.
out for me I'm com-ing too, My name's written on high.
serve my Je-sus till I die, My name's written on high.
Let God's children take the field, My name's written on high.
Christ has bought your lib-er-ty, My name's written on high.

O LAMB, BEAUTIFUL LAMB

O Lamb, beau-ti-ful Lamb! I'm going to serve God till I die;

O Lamb, beau-ti-ful Lamb! I'm going to serve God till I die

Down on my knees when the light passed by, I'm going to serve God till I die,
Nev - er felt such love be-fore, I'm going to serve God till I die,
Nev - er felt such love be-fore, I'm going to serve God till I die,
Looked at my hands, and they looked new, I'm going to serve God till I die,

Tho't my soul would rise and fly, I'm going to serve God till I die.
Go in peace and sin no more, I'm going to serve God till I die.
Made me run from door to door, I'm going to serve God till I die.
Looked at my feet, and they did, too, I'm going to serve God till I die.

138

GOING HOME IN THE CHARIOT

Going home in the chariot in the morning, Going
home in the chariot in the morning, Going home in the chariot in the
morning, Going home in the chariot in the morning.

FINE

1. O— nev-er you mind what Sa-tan say, Going home in the
2. O— sin-ner-man you bet-ter— pray, Going home in the
3. O— mourn-er, O mourn-er, you must be-lieve, Going home in the

chariot in the morn-ing. He — nev-er did teach one,—
chariot in the morn-ing. For — judgment is com-ing—
chariot in the morn-ing. And the grace of God you—

D.C.

sin-ner to pray, Going home in the chariot in the morn-ing.
ev-e-ry day, Going home in the chariot in the morn-ing.
will re-ceive, Going home in the chariot in the morn-ing.

139

WANT TO GO TO HEAVEN WHEN I DIE

1. Want to go to Heav-en when I die, Want to go to Heav-en
2. Want to see my moth-er when I die, Want to see my moth-er
3. Want to see my fa-ther when I die, Want to see my fa-ther
4. Want to see my sis-ter when I die, Want to see my sis-ter
5. Want to see my Je-sus when I die, Want to see my Je-sus

when I die, Want to go to Heav-en when I die; Good
when I die, Want to go see moth-er, when I die; Good
when I die, Want to see my fa-ther, when I die; Good
when I die, Want to see my sis-ter, when I die; Good
when I die, Want to see my Je-sus, when I die; Good

Lord, when I die, Good Lord, when I die, Good Lord, when I die,
Lord,
Lord,
Lord,
Lord,

Good Lord, when I die, Good Lord, when I die.

LEADER—Shout o-ver!

O MY LITTLE SOUL

LEADER

1. I don't care where you bu-ry my bo-dy
2. You may bu-ry my body in the east of the gar-den
3. Great big stars _____ 'way up yon-der

CHORUS

Don't care where you bu-ry my bo-dy
Bu-ry my bo-dy in the east of the gar-den
Great big stars _____ 'way up yon-der

Don't care where you bu-ry my bo-dy
Bu-ry my body in the east of the gar-den
Great big stars _____ 'way up yon-der

LEADER

O my lit-tle soul's goin' to shine, shine, O my lit-tle soul's goin' to shine, shine.
All a-roun' the heav'n goin' to shine, shine, All a-roun' the heav'n goin' to shine, shine.

CHORUS

shine, shine,   shine, shine.

I'M SO GLAD

I'm so glad, I'm so glad,

I'm so glad I've been in the grave an' rose a-gain.

LEADER **CHORUS** **LEADER**

1. I'll tell you how   I the Lord   With a
2. My soul is boun' for that bright land   Been in the grave an' rose again, An'
3. I'll go to heav'n an' take my seat   An'

CHORUS **D.C.**

hung down head an' ach-in' heart.
there I'll meet that hap-py ban'.   Been in the grave an' rose again.
cast my crown at Je-sus' feet.

142

THERE'S A GREAT CAMP MEETING

mourn and ne-ver tire, mourn and ne-ver

mourn and ne-ver tire, mourn and ne-ver

tire, There's a great camp meeting in the Promise Land.

tire, There's a great camp meeting in the Promise Land.

2.   O Get you ready children

Cho——— Don't you get weary

Verse—— Get you ready children

Cho.——— Don't you get weary

Leader—— Get you ready children

Cho. ——— Don't you get weary,
           There's a great camp meeting in the Promise Land.

Leader——— For Jesus is a-coming

Cho. ——— Don't you get weary

Leader—— Jesus is a-coming

Cho. ——— Don't you get weary

Leader—— Jesus is a-coming

Cho. ——— There's a great camp meeting in the Promise Land.

REFRAIN—— Going to pray and never tire
             Pray and never tire
             Pray and never tire
             There's a great camp meeting in the Promise Land.

3. Leader __ O I feel the spirit moving
Cho. ____ Don't you get weary
Leader__ Feel the spirit moving
Cho. ____ Don't you get weary
There's a great camp meeting in the Promise Land.
Leader__ O now I'm getting happy****
Cho. ____ Don't you get weary
Leader__ Now I'm getting happy
Cho. ____ Don't you get weary
Leader__ Now I'm getting happy
Cho. ____ Don't you get weary
There's a great camp meeting in the Promise Land.
REFRAIN— Going to shout and never tire
Shout and never tire
Shout and never tire
There's a great camp meeting in the Promise Land.

* This song illustrates well the changes which take place in the melodies over a period of time. This one originally appeared in the Hampton Institute collection and later in the "Jubilee Songs," and while it is the same in form to-day there are several differences in rhythm and melody.

** Probably the best known example of the flatted seventh.

*** The term "mourn" in the spirituals has a special meaning — a sort of weird hum, and is applied to one of the features of church worship. The term "mourner" was given to a sinner attending "revivals" or camp meetings who anticipated joining the church.

**** The phrase "getting happy" was an expression denoting religious ecstasy and was generally accompanied by shouting and mourning.

SOMETIMES I FEEL LIKE A MOTHERLESS CHILE

1. Sometimes I feel like a motherless chile,
2. Sometimes I feel like I'm al - most gone,

Some-times I feel like a motherless chile,
Some-times I feel like I'm al - most gone,

Some-times I feel like a motherless chile,
Some-times I feel like I'm al - most gone,

Far, far a -way from home a - long, long ways from home.
Far, far a -way from home a - long, long ways from home.

REFRAIN

Then I get down on my knees an'

pray ___ Get down on my knees an' pray.

I BELIEVE THIS IS JESUS

LEADER

I be-lieve this is Je-sus, Come and see, come and see, O

CHORUS

Come and see, come and see

I be-lieve this is Je-sus, Come and see, come and see.

Come and see, come and see.

Verse

1. The light of God shines in His face _____, He
2. The love of God shines in His eyes _____, He
3. Did you ev-er see such love be-fore _____, Saying

Come and see, come and see

D.C.

of-fers all His pard'ning grace
tells of man-sions in the skies Come and see, come and see.
"Go in peace and sin no more"

Come and see, come and see.

EZEK'EL SAW THE WHEEL

E - ze - k'el saw the wheel 'Way up in the
middle o' the air, E - ze - k'el saw the wheel
'Way in the middle o' the air. The big wheel moved by
Faith, The lit - tle wheel moved by the Grace o' God, A
wheel in a wheel 'Way in the middle o' the air.

LEADER

1. Jes' let me tell you what a hy - po - crite 'll do —,
2. Watch out my sister how you walk on the cross —,
3. You say the Lord has set you free —,

CHORUS

'Way in the middle o' the air,

He'll talk a-bout me an' he'll
Yo' foot might slip an' yo'
Why don't you let yo'

talk a-bout you!
soul get lost!
neigh-bor be!

'Way in the middle o' the air. E-

D.S.

NO HIDING PLACE

There's no hid-ing place down here, There's

no hid-ing place down here,

Went to the rocks for to hide my face,
Boat-man, boat-man, row one side,

Rocks cried out, "No hid-ing place," There's no hid-ing place down here.
Can't get to heav'n 'gainst wind and tide, There's no hid-ing place down here.

Third Verse

3. Sinner man, sinner man, better re-pent, God's going to call you to judgment. There's

149

YOU'RE MY BROTHER SO GIVE ME YOUR HAN'

It makes no dif-f'rence what church you may be-long to,   While
We may not be-long to   the same de-nom-i-na-tion,   While

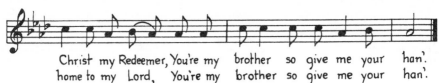

trav'lin thru this barren   lan', But   list - en   if you're workin' for
trav'lin thru this barren   lan', But   if you take me by my han'an'lead me

Christ my Redeemer, You're my   brother   so   give me your   han'.
home to my Lord,   You're my   brother so   give me your   han'.

I NEVER FELT SUCH LOVE IN MY SOUL BEFO'

I   ne-ver felt such   love   in my   soul   be-
I   ne-ver heard a   man speak like this man be-

fo'   I   ne-ver   felt   such   love   in my   soul   befo'   I   ne-ver   heard a   man speak like this man be-

fo' All the   days   of   my   life   ev - er   since   I been
fo' All the   days   of   my   life   ev - er   since   I been

born, I   ne-ver felt such   love   in my   soul   be - fo'.
born, I   ne-ver heard a   man speak like this man be - fo'.

NEW BORN AGAIN

I found free grace an'- dy-ing love, I'm new-born a-gain, Been
I know my Lord has set me free, I'm new-born a-gain, Been
My Sav-iour died for you and me, I'm new-born a-gain, Been

long time a-talk-ing 'bout my tri-als here be-low, Free grace, free grace,

free grace. Sin-ner, Free grace, free grace, I'm new-born a-gain. So glad! so glad! I'm

new-born a-gain, Been long time a-talk-ing 'bout my tri-als here be-low.

CAN'T YOU LIVE HUMBLE?

Can't you live hum-ble? Praise King Je-sus!

Can't you live hum-ble To the dy-ing Lamb?

1. Lightning flashes, thunders roll,   Make me think of my poor soul.
2. Come here, Je-sus, come here, please,   See me, Je-sus, on my knees.
3. Ev-'ry-bo-dy come and see,   A man's been here from Gal-i-lee;
4. Came down here and talked to me,   Went a-way and left me free.

SWING LOW

Swing low, sweet char-i-ot, Com-ing for to car-ry me home, Swing low, sweet char-i-ot, Com-ing for to car-ry me home.

FINE

I looked o - - ver Jor-dan, and what did I see,
If you get there be - - fore I do,
I'm some - times up, I'm some -times down,

Com-ing for to car-ry me home? A band of an-gels
Com-ing for to car-ry me home? Tell all my freinds I'm
Com-ing for to car-ry me home? But still my soul feels

com-ing af -ter me, Com-ing for to car-ry me home.
com - ing too, Com-ing for to car-ry me home.
heav-en-ly bound, Com-ing for to car-ry me home.

GO DOWN 'N THE VALLEY AND PRAY

O LORD I'M HUNGRY

O Lord I'm hungry I want to be fed,
O Lord I'm naked I want to be clothed,
O Lord I'm sin-ful I want to be saved,

O Lord__ I'm hungry I want to be fed, O
O Lord__ I'm naked I want to be clothed, O
O Lord__ I'm sin-ful I want to be sinful, O

feed me Je-sus feed me, feed me all my days, O
clothe me Je-sus clothe me, clothe me all my days, O
save me Je-sus save me, save me all my days, O

feed me Je-sus
clothe me Je-sus
save me Je-sus

feed me all the days of my life___ O feed me Je-sus feed me,
clothe me all the days of my life___ O clothe me Je-sus clothe me,
save me all the days of my life___ O save me Je-sus save me,

feed me Je-sus
clothe me Je-sus
save me Je-sus

feed me all my days, O feed me all the days of my life.
clothe me all my days, O clothe me all the days of my life.
save me all my days, O save me all the days of my life.

154

HEAR ME PRAYING

Lord, oh, hear me pray-ing, Lord, oh, hear me pray-ing,

Lord, oh, hear me pray-ing; I want to be more ho-ly ev-'ry day, oh, ev-'ry day.

Solo

1. Like Peter when you said to him, Like Peter when you said to him, Like
2. Like Peter when you said to him, Like Peter when you said to him, Like
3. Like the Baptist when you said, Like the Baptist when you said, Like

CHORUS

Feed my sheep,   Feed my sheep,
I build my church   Up-on this rock,
"I am a voice,   Crying ev-'ry day,"

Peter when you said to him,   Like   Peter when you said to him,
Peter when you said to him,   Like   Peter when you said to him,
the Baptist when you said,   Like   the Baptist when you said,

Feed my lambs,   Feed my lambs.
The gates of hell   will nev-er shock.
In the wilderness   "prepare the way."

155

I WILL PRAY

Ev-'ry time I feel the Spir-it mov-ing in my heart, I will pray.

Solo

1. When you hear me pray, my Je-sus, When you see me on my knees,
2. Je-sus died for ev-'ry sin-ner, Je-sus died for you and me,
3. Je-sus Christ, the son of Dav-id, Je-sus Christ, the Lord of all,

(Hum.)

When you hear me call-ing, Je-sus, Hear me, Je-sus, if you please.
Je-sus died for Jew and Gentile, Je-sus died up-on the tree.
Je-sus Christ, the King of heav-en, Je-sus hear me when I call.

I WISH I HAD DIED IN EGYPT LAND

"O, I can't stay a-way, I can't stay a-way, I can't

stay a-way, I wish I had died in the E-gypt land!"

FINE

1. Children grumbled on the way, "Wish I had died in the E-gypt land;"
2. Now they wept and now they moaned, "Wish I had died in the E-gypt land;"
3. Yes, the chil-dren they did right, "Wish I had died in the E-gypt land;"

Children they for-got to pray, "Wish I had died in the Egypt land." "O, I
Then they turned a-round and groaned, "Wish I had died in the Egypt land." "O, I
When they went and had that fight, "Wish I had died in the Egypt land." "O, I

D.S.

MY SINS BEEN TAKEN AWAY

1. My Lord's done ____ just what He said, ____
   My Lord's done   just what He said,
2. Some these days ____ it won't be long, ____
   Some these days   it won't be long,

Cho. *All my sins (all my sins) been tak-en a-way (been tak-en a-way),*

My Lord's done ____ just what He said;
   My Lord's done   just what He said;
Some these days ____ it won't be long;
   Some these days   it won't be long;

All my sins (all my sins) been tak-en a- way (been tak-en a-way).

My Lord's done just what He said, Healed the sick and raised the dead,
Some these days it won't be long, Go-in' home to sing my song,

All my sins been tak-en a-way, Glo-ry! glo-ry! I am saved;

All my sins been tak-en a-way, tak-en a- way.

All my sins been tak-en a- way, tak-en a- way.

HOLD THE WIND

Hold the wind! Hold the wind! Hold the wind, Don't let it blow!

Hold the wind! Hold the wind! Hold the wind, Don't let it blow!

I got my Je-sus, going to hold Him fast, Hold the wind! Don't let it blow!
I'm going to stand on a sea of glass, Hold the wind, Don't let it blow!
Thund'ring and light'ning and it looks like rain, Hold the wind, Don't let it blow!

I got my Je-sus, going to hold Him fast, Hold the wind, Don't let it blow.
I'm going to stand on a sea of glass, Hold the wind, Don't let it blow.
Thund'ring and light'ning and it looks like rain, Hold the wind, Don't let it blow.

GOOD LORD I DONE DONE

Good Lord __ I done done, Good Lord __

I done done, Good Lord __ I done done I done done what you told me to do.

FINE

LEADER   CHORUS   LEADER

1. You told me to pray and I done that too, I done done what you told me to do. I
2. You told me to mourn and I done that too,   I
3. You told me to shout and I done that too,   I

CHORUS   D.S.

prayed and prayed till I come through, I done done what you told me to do, Good
mourned and mourned till I come through,
shout and shout till I come through,

160

STAND THE STORM

O stand the storm, it won't be long, We'll an-chor bye and bye, O brethen! Stand the storm, it won't be long, We'll an-chor bye and bye.

LEADER ... CHORUS

1. My ship is on the ocean, We'll an-chor bye and
2. She's mak-ing for the kingdom, We'll an-chor bye and
3. I've a moth-er in the kingdom, We'll an-chor bye and

LEADER ... CHORUS ... D.S.

bye, My ship is on the ocean, We'll an-chor bye and bye. O
bye, She's making for the kingdom, We'll an-chor bye and bye. O
bye, I've a mother in the kingdom, We'll an-chor bye and bye. O

161

WHAT SHALL I DO?

2. Early one morning, Death came knocking at my door, etc:

3. Early one morning, Stole my mother away, etc:

4. Mother told me to meet her in Gallilee, etc:

5. Hush! Hush! Hush! The angels calling me, etc:

6. I'm so glad I got my religion in time, etc:

7. Goin' to rise and shine, Shine like a morning star, etc:

THE DOWNWARD ROAD IS CROWDED

O The down-ward road is crowd-ed, crowd-ed, crowd-ed, O the down-ward road is crowd-ed with un-be-liev-in' souls.

VERSES

1. The win' blows East, an' the win' blows West, It
blows like the judg-ment day, An' ev-'ry po' soul that
nev-er did pray, Will be glad to pray that day.

2. Some people say they believe in him
   An' then won't do what he says
   You can't ride the empty air
   An' get to heaven that day.

OLD ZION'S CHILDREN MARCHIN' ALONG

Old Zi-on's chil-dren marchin' a--long,
marchin' a-long, marchin' a-long, Old Zi-on's children marchin' a-long,

FINE LEADER
Talkin a-bout the welcome day.

1. I hailed my mother in the
2. I hailed my brother in the
3. O don't you want to live up

CHORUS   LEADER
morn- ing,
morn- ing,   marchin' a - long,   marchin' a-long,   I
yon - der,   O

D.C.
hailed my mother in the mornin'   Talkin' a-bout the welcome day.
hailed my mother in the mornin'
don't you want to live up yonder

GO DOWN MOSES

SOME OF THESE DAYS

3. I'm going down to the big baptizin',

4. I'm goin' to drink at the crystal fountain,

5. I'm goin' to sit down by my Jesus.

ALL OVER THIS WORLD

I KNOW THE LORD'S LAID HIS HANDS ON ME

O I know the Lord, I know the Lord,

I know the Lord's laid his hands on me, O hands on me.

LEADER

1. Did	ev-er	you	see	the	like	be -	fore?
	Je -	sus	preach-ing	to	the		poor.
2. O	was-	n't	that	a	hap -	py	day,
	Je -	sus	wash'd	my	sins	a -	way?
3.	Some	seek	the Lord and	don't	seek him	right,
	fool	all	day and	pray	at	night,
4.	My	Lord's	done just	what	he	said,
	healed	the	sick and	rais'd	the	dead,

CHORUS

I know the Lord's laid his hands on me, King
I know the Lord's laid his (Omit . . . .) hands on me. O
I know the Lord's laid his hands on me, When
I know the Lord's laid his (Omit. . . . . . .) hands on me. O
I know the Lord's laid his hands on me, They
I know the Lord's laid his (Omit. . . . . . .) hands on me. O
I know the Lord's laid his hands on me, He's
I know the Lord's laid his (Omit. . . . . . .) hands on me. O

168

GOT A HOME IN THAT ROCK

LEADER   **CHORUS**

I've got a home in a-that Rock, Don't you see? Don't you see?
Poor old__ Laz-'rus, poor as I Don't you see? Don't you see?

I've got a home in a-that Rock, Don't you see? Don't you see?
Poor old__ Laz-'rus, poor as I, Don't you see? Don't you see?

Be - tween the earth and sky, Thought I heard my Sav-iour cry,
Poor old Laz-'rus, poor as I When he died had a home on high.

I've got a home in a-that Rock, Don't you see? ___
He had a home in a-that Rock, Don't you see? ___

3. Rich man, Dives, lived so well, Don't you see?
   Rich man, Dives, lived so well, Don't you see?
   Rich man, Dives, lived so well, When he died he found home in hell,
   Had no home in that Rock, Don't you see?

4. God gave Noah the Rainbow sign, Don't you see?
   God gave Noah the Rainbow sign, Don't you see?
   God gave Noah the Rainbow sign, No more water but fire next time,
   Better get a home in that Rock, Don't you see?

GIVE ME YOUR HAND

O give me your hand, Give me your hand, All I want is the
love of God; Give me your hand, Give me your hand You
must be lov-ing at God's command.

1. You say you're aim-ing
2. You say the Lord has
3. Some seek God's face but

for the skies, You must be lov-ing at God's command, Why
set you free, You must be lov-ing at God's command, Why
don't seek right, You must be lov-ing at God's command, Pray

don't you quit you're tell-ing lies? You must be lov-ing at God's command.
don't you let your neighbor be? You must be lov-ing at God's command.
in the day but none at night, You must be lov-ing at God's command.

TELL ALL THE WORLD, JOHN

Tell all the world, John, Tell all the world, John,

FINE

Tell all the world, John, I know the oth-er world's not like this.

1. What kind o' shoes are those you wear, I know the oth-er world's
2. When Je - sus shook the man-na tree, I know the oth-er world's
3. Going to talk to the Fa-ther, talk to the Son, I know the oth-er world's

not like this; That you can walk up-
not like this; He shook it for you and He
not like this; Going to talk a-bout the work that I

D.C.

in the air? I know the oth-er world's not like this.
shook it for me, I know the oth-er world's not like this.
left un-done, I know the oth-er world's not like this.

RELIGION IS A FORTUNE

O re-li-gion is a for-tune, I real-ly do be-lieve;
Going to see my sis-ter Ma-ry, I real-ly do be-lieve;
Going to chat-ter with the an-gels, I real-ly do be-lieve;
Going to walk and talk with Je-sus, I real-ly do be-lieve;

1.
O re-li-gion is a for-tune, I real-ly do be-lieve.
Going to see my sis-ter Ma-ry, I real-ly do be-lieve.
Going to chat-ter with the an-gels, I real-ly do be-lieve.
Going to walk and walk with Je-sus, I real-ly do be-lieve.

2. *FINE* DUET
O Sabbaths have no end. Where've you been, poor sin-ner? Where've you been so
O Sabbaths have no end. Where've you been, poor mourner? Where've you been so
O Sabbaths have no end. Where've you been, young con-vert? Where've you been so
O Sabbaths have no end. Where've you been, good christian? Where've you been so

long? Been low down in the val-ley for to pray, And I ain't got wea-ry yet.

172

SHOUT FOR JOY

173

I'VE JUST COME FROM THE FOUNTAIN

I've just come from the fountain, I've just come from the fountain, Lord, I've just come from the fountain, His name's so sweet.

O brothers I love Jesus O brothers I love Jesus O brothers I love Jesus
O sisters I love Jesus O sisters I love Jesus O sisters I love Jesus His name's so sweet.
Been drinking from the fountain Been drinking from the fountain Been drinking from the fountain

174

THE OLD ARK'S A MOVERING

O, the old ark's a-mov-er-ing, a-mov-er-ing, a-mov-er-ing

The old ark's a-mov-er-ing, And I'm going home, O, the I'm going home.

See that sis - ter dressed so fine? She
See that broth - er dressed so gay?
See that sis - ter com - ing so slow? She
Th'aint but the one thing grieves my mind;

D.C. Sing before 1st & after 4th stanza.

ain't got Je - sus in a her mind.
Death's goin' a come for to car - ry him a-way. ⎫ Th'old ark she reeled, The
wants to go to Heav'n 'fore the Heav-en doors close. ⎭
Sis - ter's gone to Heav'n and left a me be-hind.

old ark she rocked, Old ark she land-ed on the mountain top.

175

O MARY DON'T YOU WEEP DON'T YOU MOURN

O Ma-ry, don't you weep, don't you mourn, O Ma-ry, don't you weep don't you mourn; Pha-roh's ar-my got drownd-ed, O Ma-ry, don't you weep.

Some of these morn-ings
When I get to Heaven goin' to
When I get to Heaven goin' to

bright and fair, Take my wings and cleave the air.
sing and shout, No-bod-y there for turn me out.
put on my shoes, Run a-bout glo-ry and tell all the news.

Pha-roh's ar-my got drownd-ed O Ma-ry, don't you weep.

WITNESS

LEADER CHORUS LEADER

My soul is a wit-ness for my Lord, My soul is a witness
for my Lord,

CHORUS LEADER CHORUS LEADER CHORUS

for my Lord, My soul is a wit-ness for my Lord, My soul is a wit-ness for my Lord.
for my Lord, for my Lord,

STANZA

Hum

You read in the Bi-ble and you un-der-stand, Me-thu-se-lah was the

old-est man, He lived nine hundred and ninety nine, He died and went to Heaven, Lord,

in a-due time. Now Me-thuselah was a wit-ness for my Lord, Me-
Samson was a wit-ness for my Lord,

thusaleh was a wit-ness for my Lord, Me-
Sam-son was a wit-ness (Omit _ _ _ _ _) for my Lord.

STANZA

Hum

2. You read in the Bi-ble and you understand, Sam-son went out at a-one time And he
Sam-son was the strongest man; li-lah fooled Samson, this we know, For the

Hum

killed a-bout a thousand of the Phil-is-tines. De-
ho - ly Bi-ble ___ tells us so. She shaved off his head just as

clean as your hand, And his strength became as a- ny oth-er man's.

STANZA

Hum

3. Now Dan-iel was a He-brew child, He went to pray to his Lord awhile, The

Hum

King at once for Daniel did send, And he put him right down in the li-ons' den;

rit. **All sing words.**

God sent His angels the li-ons for to keep, And Dan-iel lay down and

went to sleep. Now Dan-iel was a wit-ness for my Lord, Now
Who will be a wit-ness for my Lord?

Dan-iel was a wit-ness for my Lord, Daniel was a wit-ness for my Lord,
Who will be a wit-ness for my Lord? Who will be a wit-ness for my Lord?

1. Dan-iel was a wit-ness for my Lord. **2.** Who will be a wit-ness for my Lord?

ff Molto rit.

GOING TO SHOUT ALL OVER GOD'S HEAV'N

* Let the last syllable of heav'n be a hum.

MARCHNG UP THE HEAVENLY ROAD

Marching up the heav-en-ly road,

Marching up the heav-en-ly road, I'm bound to fight un-til I die;

Marching up the heav - en - ly road. road.

LEADER

My sis-ter, have you got your sword and shield, Marching up the heav-en-ly road, I
O come a-long —Mos-es, don't get lost, Marching up the heav-en-ly road, I
O fare you well friends, fare you well foes, Marching up the heav-en-ly road, I

got 'em fo' I left the field, Marching up the heav-en-ly road.
stretch your rod and come a - cross, Marching up the heav-en-ly road.
leave you all my eyes to close, Marching up the heav-en-ly road.

GREAT DAY

Great day! Great day, the righteous marching. Great day.

1. / **FINE** / **2.** / Solo

God's going to build up Zi-on's walls, Zi-on's walls ___

1. Cha - riot rode on the mountain top,
2. This is the day of ju - bi - lee,
3. We want no cow - ards in our band,
4. Going to take my breast-plate, sword and shield,

Solo

God's going to build up Zi-on's walls!

My God spoke and the chariot did stop,
The Lord has set His peo - ple free,
We call for va - li - ant heart - ed men,
And march out bold-ly in the field,

D.C.

God's	going	to	build	up	Zi	-	on's	walls!
God's	going	to	build	up	Zi	-	on's	walls!
God's	going	to	build	up	Zi	-	on's	walls!
God's	going	to	build	up	Zi	-	on's	walls!

I HEARD THE PREACHING OF THE ELDER

I heard the preaching of the El-der, Preaching the Word,

preach-ing the Word; I heard the preach-ing of the El-der,

Preaching the Word of God.

FINE

1. How long did it rain? Can
2. How long was Jon-ah in the
3. When I was a mourn-er

any one tell? Preaching the Word of God. For for-ty
bel-ly of the whale? Preaching the Word of God, Three whole
just like you, Preaching the Word of God, My knees got ac-

days and nights it fell, Preaching the Word of God.
days and nights he sailed, Preaching the Word of God.
quaint-ed with the hill-sides too, Preaching the Word of God.

LIVE A HUMBLE

Live a hum-ble, hum-ble, Humble yourselves the

bells done rung, Live a bell's done rung. Glory and hon-or! Praise King Jesus!

Glo-ry and hon-or! Praise the Lord! Praise the Lord! Live a-

Verse

(1.) Watch that sun, how steady he runs, Don't let him catch you with your work undone. Live a

Verse

(2) Ev-er see such a man as God? He gave up his Son for to come and die. Gave up his Son for to come and die, Just to save my soul from a burning fire, Live a-

Verse

(3) See God 'n' you see God 'n' you see God in the morning, He'll come rid-ing down the line of time; The fire'll be fall-ing, He'll be call-ing, "Come to judg-e-ment come," Liv-a-

AIN'T I GLAD I'VE GOT OUT THE WILDERNESS

1. O, ain't I glad I've got out the wil-der-ness, Got out the wil-der-ness, got out the wil-der-ness, Ain't I glad I've got out the wil-der-ness, Leaning on the Lord. O, ain't I glad I've Lord.

2. O, come along, mourner, run out the wil-der-ness, Run out the wil-der-ness, run out the wil-der-ness, Come a-long mourn-er, run out the wil-der-ness, Leaning on the Lord. O, come along, mourner, Lord.

3. O, you're long time, mourner, coming out the wil-der-ness, Coming out the wil-der-ness, com-ing out the wil-der-ness, Long time mourn-er, coming out the wil-der-ness, Leaning on the Lord. O, long time mourner, Lord.

4. O, ain't I glad I've got out the wil-der-ness, Got out the wil-der-ness, got out the wil-der-ness, Ain't I glad I got out the wil-der-ness, Leaning on the Lord. O, ain't I glad I Lord.

REFRAIN

Come a-lean-ing on the Lord, Come a-lean-ing on the Lord, Come a-lean-ing on the Lamb of God that takes a-way the sin of the world.

I HAVE ANOTHER BUILDING

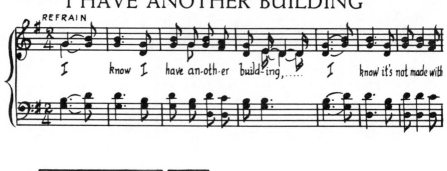

I AM THE TRUE VINE

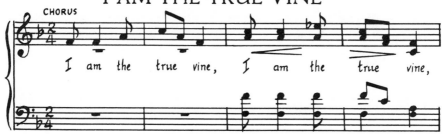

CHORUS

I am the true vine, I am the true vine,

FINE

I am the true vine, My Fa-ther is the hus-band-man.

1. I am in Him, and He's in me, My Fa-ther is the husband-man,
2. I know my Lord has set me free, My Fa-ther is the husband-man,
3. I know my Lord is kind and true, My Fa-ther is the husband-man,

D.C.

Ev - 'ry day He comforts me, My Fa-ther is the hus-band-man.
I'm in Him and He's in me, My Fa-ther is the hus-band-man.
For He loves me, and He loves you, My Fa-ther is the hus-band-man.

PLENTY GOOD ROOM

There's plen-ty good room, There's plen-ty good room, Way in the

king-dom; There's plen-ty good room, There's plen-ty good room,

Way in the kingdom.

1. My Lord's done just what he said, Way in the
2. One of these mornings bright and fair, Way in the
3. When I was a mourner just like you, Way in the
4. Come on, mourner make a bound, Way in the

king-dom; Healed the sick and raised the dead, Way in the king-dom.
king-dom; Going to hitch on my wings and cleave the air, Way in the king-dom.
king-dom; I prayed and prayed till I came thro', Way in the king-dom.
king-dom; The Lord will meet you on half way ground, Way in the king-dom.

NOBODY KNOWS WHO I AM

O, no-bod-y knows a who I am, a who I am, till the judg-ment morn-ing! Heav'n bells a-ring-ing, the saints all a-sing-ing, Heav'n bells a-ring-ing in my soul, O, the soul.

1. Want to go to Heav-en, Want to go right,
2. Don't want to stum-ble, Don't want to fall,
3. If you don't be-lieve that I've been re-deemed,

Want to go to Heav-en All dressed in white. The
Want to be in Heav-en When the roll is called. The
fol-low me down......... To Jor-dan's stream. The

189

LET US CHEER THE WEARY TRAVELLER

Let us cheer the wea-ry trav-el-ler,..... Cheer the wea-ry trav-el-ler

FINE

Let us cheer the wea-ry trav-el-ler, A - long the heaven-ly way.

1. I'll take my gos-pel trum-pet, And I'll be-gin to blow,
2. And if you meet with cross- es And tri-als on the way,

D.C.

And if my Sav-iour helps me, I'll blow wher-ev-er I go.
Just keep your trust in Je-sus, And don't for-get to pray.

3. If you cannot sing like Angels
If you cannot pray like Paul
You can tell the love of Jesus
And say he died for all.

SINNER PLEASE DON'T LET THIS HARVEST PASS

CHORUS

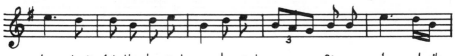

Sin-ner, please don't let this har-vest pass;............ Sin-ner, har-vest pass;

please don't let this har-vest pass, har-vest pass; Sin-ner, please don't

FINE

let this har-vest pass, and die and lose your soul at last........ soul at last.

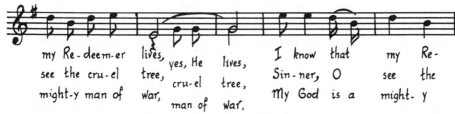

1. I know that my Re-deem-er lives,............ I know that
   yes, He lives;
2. Sin-ner, O see the cru-el tree,............ Sin-ner, O
   cru-el tree,
3 My God is a might-y man of war, My God is a
   man of war,

my Re-deem-er lives, yes, He lives, I know that my Re-
see the cru-el tree, cru-el tree, Sin-ner, O see the
might-y man of war, man of war, My God is a might-y

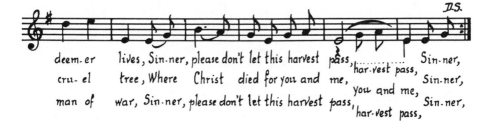

D.S.

deem-er lives, Sin-ner, please don't let this harvest pass,............ Sin-ner,
har-vest pass,
cru-el tree, Where Christ died for you and me, Sin-ner,
you and me,
man of war, Sin-ner, please don't let this harvest pass, Sin-ner,
har-vest pass,

191

SOMEBODY'S KNOCKING AT YOUR DOOR

Somebody's knocking at your door, Somebody's knocking at your door,

O.... sin-ner, why don't you an-swer? Somebody's knocking at your door.

1. Knocks like Je - sus Some - bod - y's knocking at your
2. Can't you hear Him? Some - bod - y's knocking at your
3. An - swer Je - sus, Some - bod - y's knocking at your
4. Je - sus calls you, Some - bod - y's knocking at your
5. Can't you trust Him? Some - bod - y's knocking at your

door. Knocks like Je - sus, Some - bod - y's knocking at your door.
door. Can't you hear Him? Some - bod - y's knocking at your door.
door. An - swer Je - sus, Some - bod - y's knocking at your door.
door. Je - sus calls you, Some - bod - y's knocking at your door.
door. Can't you trust Him? Some - bod - y's knocking at your door.

POOR SINNER

Refrain.— O poor sin-ner, O now is your time. O poor sin-ner, O,
What you goin' to do when your lamp burns down? 1. Fire in the east,
fire in the west, What you goin' to do when your lamp burns down? Fire goin' to
burn up the wil-der-ness, What you goin' to do when your lamp burns down?

2. Head got wet with midnight dew,
   What you goin' to do when your lamp burns down?
   Morning star was witness, too,
   What you goin' to do when your lamp burns down?

3. Wind blows hard, wind blows cold. What you goin' to do, etc.
   Lord, have mercy on my soul. What you goin' to do, etc.

4. I done died, don't die no more, What you goin' to do, etc.
   I'm goin' to cross on the other shore, What you goin', etc.

POOR MOURNER'S GOT A HOME

AIN'T THAT GOOD NEWS?

1. I've a crown up in the Kingdom, Ain't that good news! I've a crown up in the
2. I've a harp up in the Kingdom, Ain't that good news! I've a harp up in the
3. I've a robe up in the Kingdom, Ain't that good news! I've a robe up in the
4. I've slippers in the Kingdom, Ain't that good news! I've slippers in the
5. I've a Saviour in the Kingdom, Ain't that good news! I've a Saviour in the

Kingdom, Ain't that good news! I'm a-goin' to lay down this world, Goin' to

shoulder up my cross, Goin' to take it home to Je-sus, Ain't that good news!

In this collection there are three different songs with practically the same melody : "Ain't that good news".—"Death ain't nothing but a robber", and "I got a home in-a that Rock".

195

I'M AGOING TO JOIN THE BAND

LEADER

Hal-le-lu - jah! ... Can't you sing it ..

I'm-a going to join the band, I'm-a going to join the band,

✳ O Lord.

I'm-a going to join the band, I'm-a going to join the band.

FINE

1. The more come in with a free good-will,
2. Jordan's stream is so chil - ly and cold, If
3. Watch that Sun, how stead-y she runs;
4. Josh-u-a prayed for to stop the sun, The
5. Going to hang my harp on the wil - low tree, It'll

Make the band seem sweet-er still. And
you don't mind it'll chill your soul. And
Don't let her catch you with your work un - done. And
Sun did stop till the bat-tle was won. And
sound way o - ver in Gal - i - lee And

D.C.

Exclamations for Verses.

1. Come children!
   Join the band!
   Sing to Jesus!

2. Cold Jordan!
   Chilly waters!
   Watch it, Christians!

3. Watch that Sun!
   Steady, traveler!
   Work, children!

4. Going to heaven!
   With Joshua!
   And David!

5. O the willow!
   And the children!
   Couldn't sing!

The chorus in this song, as in "This is a Sin-trying World" and "My Soul's been Anchored in the Lord," is continuous, while the leader interjects whatever exclamations seem to him appropriate.

✳ These exclamations are not the only ones that can be used. Any others which seem suitable and do not destroy the rhythm may be employed.

FREE AT LAST

Free at last, free at last, I thank God I'm free at last; Free at last,

Free at last,..... I thank God I'm free at last. O free at last.

1. 'Way down yonder in the grave-yard walk, I thank God I'm
2. On a my knees when the light pass'd by, I thank God I'm
3. Some of these morn-ings, bright and fair, I thank God I'm

free at last,.... Me and my Je-sus goin' to
free at last,.... Tho't... my soul.. would...
free at last, Goin' meet... King Je.... sus......

meet and talk,... I thank God I'm free at last, O
rise and fly,..... I thank God I'm free at last, O
in the air,..... I thank God I'm free at last,

I'VE DONE WHAT YOU TOLD ME TO DO

1. O Lord, I've done what you told me to do,   O Lord, I've
2. O Ga-briel, come on... down the line,   O Ga-briel,

done what you told me to do, ... O Lord, I've
come on.... down.. the line, ... O Ga-briel

done what you told me to do, In a-that
come on.... down... the line, In a-that

morn-ing, O my Lord, In a-that morn-ing, O my Lord, In a-that

morning when the Lord says "Hur-ry!" In... a-that "Hur-ry!"

3. O gambler, you can't get on a-this train? etc.
4. O sister, have you got your ticket signed? etc.

ROLL, JORDAN, ROLL

Roll Jordan roll! Roll Jordan roll, I want to go to heaven when I die, To hear old Jordan roll.

Leader
1. O brother you ought to been there
2. O sister you aught to been there
3. O seeker you ought to been there

Chorus
Yes my Lord,

Leader
A- sitting in the kingdom,
A- sitting in the kingdom, To hear old Jordan roll.
A- sitting in the kingdom,

199

I'M A-GOING TO DO ALL I CAN

2. I'm a-going to pray all I can
3. I'm a-going to bear all I can
4. I'm a-going to sing all I can

* *To be pronounced as one syllable.*

DONE MADE MY VOW TO THE LORD

Done made my vow to the Lord and I ne-ver will turn back, I will go, I shall go to see what the end will be. Done opened my mouth to the Lord and I never will turn back, I will go, I shall go to see what the end will be.

FINE

Leader
1. Some-
2. I'll
3. If

Chorus

Leader

times I'm up, sometimes I'm down,
pray and pray and nev-er stop,
you get there be-fore I do,

see what the end will be,

But
Un-
Tell

Chorus

D.S.

still my soul is heav'nly bound,
til I reach the mountain top,
all my friends I'm coming too,

See what the end will be. Done

STUDY WAR NO MORE

I'm a-going to lay down my sword and shield

Down by the riv-er-side, down by the river-side,

down by the riv-er-side, Going to lay down my sword and shield,

Down by the riv-er-side, Ain't going to study ___ war no

* *To be pronounced as one syllable.*

2. I'm a-going to put on my long white robe
   Down by the riverside, down by the riverside, down by the riverside.
   I'm a-going to put on my long white robe
   Down by the riverside.
   Ain't going to study war no more. Refrain.

3. I'm a-going to talk with the Prince of Peace.

* To be pronounced as one syllable.

203

MARCH ON

IS THERE ANYBODY HERE?

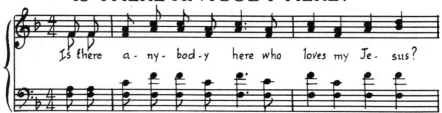

Is there a-ny-bod-y here who loves my Je-sus?

A-ny-bod-y here who loves my Lord? I want to know if you

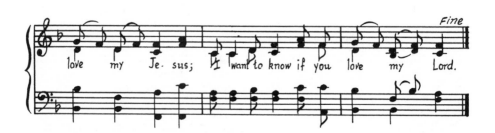

love my Je-sus; I want to know if you love my Lord.

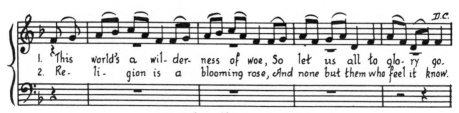

1. This world's a wil-der-ness of woe, So let us all to glo-ry go.
2. Re-li-gion is a blooming rose, And none but them who feel it know.

3. When I was blind and could not see,
   King Jesus brought the light to me.

4. When ev'ry star refuse to shine,
   I know King Jesus will be mine

206

THERE'S ROOM ENOUGH

1. O brothers,   brothers,
2. O sinners,   sinners,
3. O mourners,   mourners,

CHORUS

Don't stay a-way! _____ Don't

O brothers,
O sinners,
O mourners,

stay a-way _____ Don't stay a-way, don't stay a-way, for my Lord says there's room e-nough, Room e-nough in the heav'n for us all, my Lord says there's room enough, So don't stay a-way.

TRYIN' TO CROSS THE RED SEA

Did-n't ol' Pharoah get lost, get lost, get lost,

Did-n't ol' Pharoah get lost, yes *tryin' to cross the Red Sea.

Creep a-long Moses, Moses creep a-long, Creep a-long Moses I thank God.

FINE

Leader
1. I went down in the valley an' I did-n't go to stay,
2. I went down in the valley to of-fer up prayer,
3. Ol' Sa-tan's mad an' I am glad,
4. I wonder what ol' Sa-tan's grumb-lin' a-bout,

Chorus
* Tryin' to cross the Red Sea,

Leader
My soul got happy an' I
when I got there ol'
He missed that soul he
He's down in hell an'

stayed all day
Satan was there
thought he had
can't get out

Chorus
* Tryin' to cross the Red Sea.

* To be pronounced as one syllable.

LISTEN TO THE ANGELS SHOUTIN'

Leader

1. Where do you think I foun' my soul,
2. 'Way ov-er yonder by Jor-dan's stream,

I foun' my soul at hell's dark door,
I hear them shoutin' "I've been re-deemed"

Be-fore I'd lay in
If you get there be-

hell one day,
fore I do,

I'd
Tell

Chorus

Listen to the an-gels shoutin',

Listen to the angels shoutin'.

List-en to the angels shoutin'

HALLELUJAH

Halle - lu - jah! hal - le lu - jah!

I do be - long to that ban', hal - le - lu!

Leader

1. I have a sis - ter, in that day ___
2. I nev - er shall for - get that day ___ When
3. Looked at my han's an my han's looked new ___
4. I nev - er felt such love be - fore Sayin'

She'll take wings an' fly a - way.
Je - sus washed my sins a - way.
Looked at my feet an' they looked so too.
"Go in peace an' sin no more.

Chorus

I do be - long to the ban' hal - le - lu!

YOU'D BETTER MIN'

Leader

1. You'd better min' how you talk, you'd better min' what you talk about,
2. You'd better min' how you sing, you'd better min' what you sing about, For you
3. You'd better min' how you shout, you'd better min' what you shout about,

got to give ac.count in Judgment, You'd bet-ter min'. You'd better

min', You'd better min', For you
You'd bet-ter min', You'd better min',

got to give ac.count in Judgment, You'd bet-ter min'.

RUN, MOURNER, RUN

Verses

1. There's singing here, There's singing there, I I be-
   lieve down in my soul there's singing ev'-ry-where.
2. There's preaching here, There's preaching there, I I be-
   lieve down in my soul there's preach-ing ev'-ry-where.
3. There's praying here, There's praying there, I be-
   lieve down in my soul there's pray-ing ev'-ry-where.

Chorus

Run mourner run! Lo! says the bi-ble,

Run mour-ner run, Lo! is the way.

EV'RY DAY'LL BE SUNDAY

Refrain

Bye an' bye, bye an' bye, good Lord! Bye and bye, Ev'-ry day'll be Sun-day bye an' bye

Fine — **Verses**

1. One o' these morn-in's bright an' fair,
2. One day, one day as I's walkin' a-long,

Chorus — **Leader**

Ev'-ry day'll be Sunday bye an' bye, Goin' to take my wings an' thought I heard the

cleave the air, Ev'-ry day'll be Sun-day bye an' bye. **D. C.**
an-gels song,

GLORY TO THAT NEWBORN KING

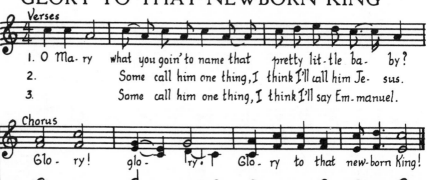

Verses

1. O Ma-ry what you goin' to name that pretty lit-tle ba-by?
2. Some call him one thing, I think I'll call him Je- sus.
3. Some call him one thing, I think I'll say Em-manuel.

Chorus

Glo-ry! glo-ry! Glo-ry to that new-born King!

WASN'T THAT A MIGHTY DAY

1. Wasn't that a might-y day, Wasn't that a
2. Star rose in the east Star rose

might-y day, wasn't that a might-y
in the east, Star rose in the

day, When Je-sus Christ was born.
east, When Je-sus Christ was born.

GO TELL IT ON THE MOUNTAIN

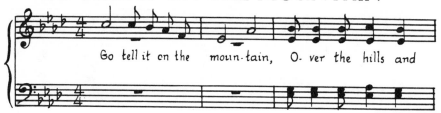

Go tell it on the moun-tain, O- ver the hills and

ev- er- y - where, Go tell it on the

moun - tain that Je- sus Christ is born.

Verses *

1. While shepherds kept their watching o'er si- lent flocks by
2. The shepherds feared and trembled when lo! a- bove the
3. Down in a lone ly manger the hum-ble Christ was

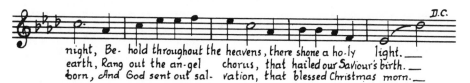

night, Be- hold throughout the heavens, there shone a ho-ly light. __
earth, Rang out the an-gel chorus, that hailed our Saviour's birth. __
born, And God sent out sal- vation, that blessed Christmas morn. __

* *These verses were supplied by John Work Sr. in place of the original
ones which could not be found.*

HE'S GOT HIS EYES ON YOU

He's got His eyes on you, He's got His
eyes on you. My Lord's sittin' in the
King-dom, He's got His eyes on you.

Verses

1. I would not be a sin-ner,
2. I would not be a gambler,
3. I would not be a li-ar,   I tell you the reason

why   'fraid my Lord might call   me, An' I

wouldn't be   ready   to   die.

MY LORD'S GOIN' MOVE THIS WICKED RACE

My Lord's, my Lord's, goin' move this wicked race ____ this wick-ed
Lord, Lord
race, this wick-ed race, My Lord's goin' move this wicked
race, He's goin' to raise up a nation that shall o bey! *Fine*

Verses

1. Ni-co-de-mus
2. Marvel not man

1. Nicode-mus he de-sired to know, de-sired to
2. Marvel not man if you want to be wise, if you want to be
Lord, Lord
know, de-sired to know, ni-co-de-mus he de-sired to
wise, if you want to be wise, Marvel not man if you want to be

D.C. after 3rd Verse.

know, How can a man be born when he is old?
wise, Just be-lieve on Jesus and be bap-tized!

3. God called old Moses on the mountain top, on the mountain top, on the mountain top,
   God called old Moses on the mountain top
   And He stamped His law on Moses' heart.

217

HE IS KING OF KINGS

He is king of kings, He is Lord of Lords,

Je- sus Christ the first and last, No man works like him.

Leader

1. He built his throne up in the air,
2. He pitched his tents on Ca- naan's ground

Chorus   Leader

No man works like him, And called his saints from
                                And broke the Ro- man

Chorus

ev- 'ry- where,   No man works like him.
king- dom down,

THERE'S A MEETING HERE TONIGHT

219

meet-ing here to-night. Get you read-y, there's a

meet-ing here to-night.

WE ARE CLIMBING JACOB'S LADDER

Leader ... Chorus

1. We are climbing Ja-cob's ladder, we are
2. Ev-ry round goes high-er'n' higher Ev'-ry
3. Brother do you love my Je-sus Bro-ther

climbing Ja-cob's lad-der, We are
round goes high-er'n' high-er, Ev'-ry
do you love my Je-sus, Bro-ther

climbing Ja-cob's lad-der
round goes high-er'n' high-er
do you love my Je-sus

sol-dier of the Cross.
sol-dier of the Cross.
sol-dier of the Cross.

4. If you love him why not serve him

I'M JUST A-GOIN' OVER THERE

I'm just a. go in' 'way o ver Jor-dan, I'm just a-
go-in' o-ver there, I'm go-in' home to see my
brother,
mother, I'm just a. go in' over there.
Jesus,
I'm just a- go in' over Jordan, I'm just a-
go in' over there, I'm go in' home to see my
brother
mother I'm just a. go in' o-ver there.
Je-sus

221

THERE'S SOMETHING ON MY MIND

1. There's somethin' on my mind that's worryin' me, There's somethin' on my mind that's worryin' me, There's somethin' on my mind that's worryin' me So let us watch Lord an' pray as we live.

2. Father's drinkin' with their sons that's what's worryin' me, Fathers drinkin' with their sons that's what worryin' me, Fathers drinkin' with their sons that's what worryin' me So

3. The church is out of union that's what's worryin' me
The church is out of union that's what's worryin' me
The church is out of union that's what's worryin' me
So let us watch Lord, an' pray as we live.

THE LORD IS MY SHEPHERD

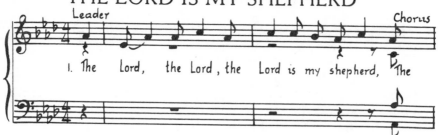

1. The Lord, the Lord, the Lord is my shepherd, The
Lord, the Lord, the Lord is my shepherd, the Lord, the Lord, the
Lord is my shepherd The Lord is my shepherd and I shall not want.

2. He makes me to lie down in green pastures,
   He maketh me to lie down in green pastures,
   He maketh me to lie down in green pastures,
   The Lord is my shepherd and I shall not want.

3. He leadeth me beside the still water,
   He leadeth me beside the still water,
   He leadeth me beside the still water,
   The Lord is my shepherd and I shall not want.

GOT MY LETTER

Got my let-ter Got my let-ter

Got my let-ter goin' to hail the train Got my letter, got my

let-ter, got my let-ter Got my let-ter goin' to hail the train.

Verse

1. Fisher-man Pe-ter out on the
2. I got my re-li-gion from out the

sea stop yo' fish-in' Pe-ter
sun I clapped my hands

come and fol-low me.
an' be-gan to run.

3. You can weep like a willow
You can mourn like a dove
But you can't get to heaven
without Christian love.

224

SEE THE SIGNS OF JUDGMENT

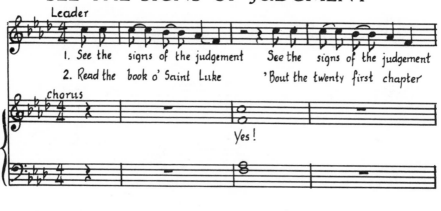

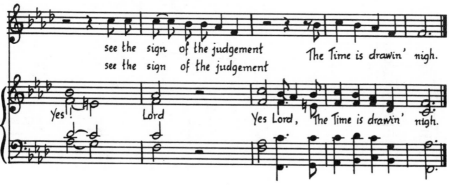

HALLELU

I'M GOIN' TO SING

I'm goin' to {sing/pray/shout} when the spirit says {sing/pray/shout} I'm goin' to {sing/pray/shout} when the spirit says {sing/pray/shout} I'm goin' to {sing/pray/shout} when the spirit says shout {sing/pray/shout} An' o-bey the spirit of the Lord.

ROCKIN' JERUSALEM

O Mary O Martha O Mary ring dem bells. I hear arch angels a-rockin' Je-ru-sa-lem, I hear arch angels a- ring-in' dem bells.

Fine *Leader*
1. Church gettin' high-er!
2. List-en to the lambs!
3. New Je-ru-sa-lem!

Chorus *Leader* *Chorus D.C.*
Rockin' Je-ru-sa-lem! Church gettin' higher Ring-a dem bells.
Listen to the lambs
New Je-ru-sa-lem

KING JESUS BUILT ME A HOUSE ABOVE

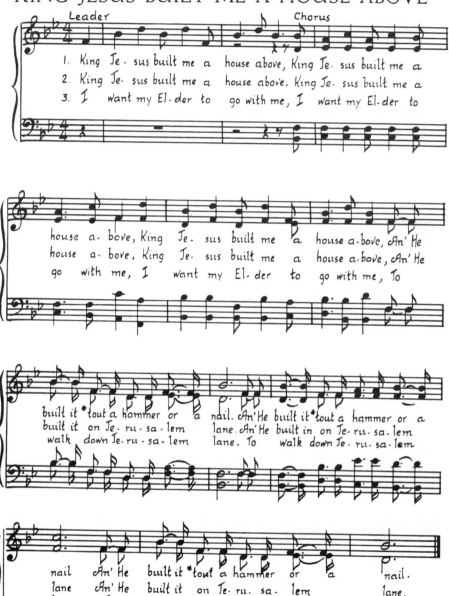

1. King Je-sus built me a house above, King Je-sus built me a house a-bove, King Je-sus built me a house a-bove, An' He built it *tout a hammer or a nail. An' He built it *tout a hammer or a nail An' He built it *tout a hammer or a nail.

2. King Je-sus built me a house above, King Je-sus built me a house a-bove, An' He built it on Je-ru-sa-lem lane. An' He built in on Je-ru-sa-lem lane. An' He built it on Je-ru-sa-lem lane.

3. I want my El-der to go with me, I want my El-der to go with me, To walk down Je-ru-sa-lem lane. To walk down Je-ru-sa-lem lane. To walk down Je-ru-sa-lem lane.

* without

4. I want my sister to go with me
To feast on the heavenly manna.

BYE AND BYE

Bye an' bye we all shall meet a-gain Bye an' bye we

all shall meet a-gain, O Bye an' bye we

all shall meet a-gain, An' I wouldn't mind dyin' if dyin' was all.

2. After death got to fill an empty grave
   After death got to fill an empty grave
   After death got to fill an empty grave
   An' I wouldn't mind dyin' if dyin' was all.

THE SUN MOWS DOWN

229

GOD'S GOIN' TO STRAIGHTEN THEM

We got deacons in de church
We got preachers in de church Dey ain't straight Who's goin' to
We got members in de church

straighten them
God's goin' to straighten them
He says He's goin'to straighten them, God's goin' to

straighten all de peo-ple in His church.

HE'S A MIGHTY GOOD LEADER

He's a mighty good leader ____ He's a mighty good leader ____ He's a mighty good leader, Je - sus Christ God's Son ____ God's Son, God's Son, He's a mighty good leader ____ He's a mighty good lead ____ er, He's a mighty good leader, Je - sus Christ, God's Son.

2. He is my Captain
3. In the time of trouble.

231

O IT'S GOIN' TO BE A MIGHTY DAY

Verses

1. Yes the book of Re-ve-la-tions to be brought forth on that day
   An' ev'-ry leaf un-folded the book of the seven seals.

2. As I went down into E-gypt I camped up-on the groun'.
   At the soundin' of the trumpet the Ho-ly Ghost came down.

3. The good ol' chariot passing by
   She jarred the earth an' shook the sky.

4. I ain't got time for to stop an' talk
   The road is rough an' it's hard to walk.

232

JOHN HENRY

This ol' hammer killed John Henry! This ol' hammer killed John
This ol' hammer shines like silver! This ol' hammer shines like

Henry! This ol' hammer killed John Henry, But this ol' hammer won't kill me!
silver! This ol' hammer shines like silver, But rings like gol', rings like gol!

3. Take my hammer to the walkin' boss
Take my hammer to the walkin' boss
Take my hammer to the walkin' boss
Tell 'im I'm gone, tell 'im I'm gone.

4. If he ask you any questions
If he ask you any questions
If he ask you any questions
You don't know, tell 'im you don't know.

JOHN HENRY

(SECOND VERSION)

This is the hammer that killed John Henry, This is the

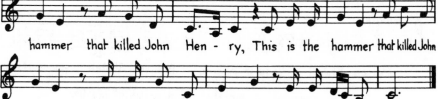

hammer that killed John Hen - ry, This is the hammer that killed John

Hen-ry But it won't kill me, Lord, But it won't kill me.

CONVICT SONG (1)

Lawd I wonder if I'll ever get back home, get back home

CONVICT SONG (2)

1. Ev - 'ry mail day ——— I get a
2. I got a let - ter from my ol - des
3. One of these morn - ins goin home to my
4. Go tell my ba - by to keep on a-

let-ter, says "Son come home" —— says "Son come home."
broth-er says "Son come home" —— says "Son come home."
mammy I'm go - in' home" —— Yes I'm go - in' home."
wait-in' For I'm com - in' home" —— Yes I'm com - in' home.

BET ON STUBALL

Ol' Stuball fastes' race horse, He goes 'roun like show'rin' rain.

REFRAIN

Bet on Stuball you might win, Bet on Stuball you might win.

2. O marster, o marster, I'm a-riskin' my life
Tryin' to win you a fortune for you an' yo' wife. Refrain.

234

HOT BOILIN' SUN COMIN' OVER

1. _____ Look-a yon-der! Hot boilin' sun comin'
2. Thought you wasn't com-in', Thought you wasn't comin' this

yon - der
com - in'

o - ver, Thought you wasn't Look-a look-a yon - der,
morn - in', wasn't com - in'

Hot boil - in' sun, com-in' o - ver An' he
Thought you wasn't comin' this mornin' But you're

ain't goin' down _____ An' he ain't goin' down.
here on time _____ But you're here on time.

3. I got a mule,
   I got a mule named Jerry,
   I got a mule,
   I got a mule named Jerry,
   An' he's mine, all mine,
   Lawd he's mine, all mine.

4. I can ride him,
   I can ride him when I want to,
   I can ride him,
   I can ride him when I want to,
   If it's all day long,
   If it's all day long.

CAPTAIN SAYS HURRY

Captain says "hurry! Straw boss says "run!" I got a good no-tion not to do nar' one.

2. Captain on the hook team, skid on the plow
   Head-knocker jumpin' on the Johnson bar.

3. Befo' I'd drive a six mule team
   I'd drink my water from a runnin' stream.

4. Shot five dollars, the point was nine
   Six spot toppin' an' the three come flyin'.

5. Come here Baby what's on yo' min'?
   "Can't sleep fo' dreamin' can't stay 'wake fo' cryin'.

6. Knocked on her window, rapped on her do'
   She gave me a col' answer an' tol' me to go.

7. Mean ol' fireman, cruel ol' engineer
   Took my brownskin an' lef' me standin' here.

8. I'm standin' here wond'rin' will a match-box hol' my clothes
   Ain't got no money, an' got so far to go.

CAPTAIN, O CAPTAIN

Captain,   O   captain,   you   must be ___
cross,   It's   six   o'clock   an' you won't "knock-off!"

2. Captain, O captain you must be blin'
   You keep hollerin' "hurry" an' I'm darn nigh flyin'.

3. Woke up this mornin' feelin' mighty mean
   Thinkin' 'bout my good gal in New Orleans.

4. One o' these mornins it won't be long
   You goin' holler fo' me but I'll be gone.

5. Wouldn't min' marryin' but I can't stan' settlin' down
   Goin' act like a preacher an' ride from town to town.

6. If I feel tomorrow like I feel today
   Goin' pack my suit-case an' make my get-away.

7. Stoop down boys an' pick up strong
   Pay day's comin' an it won't be long.

8. Go tell the fireman to keep the boilers hot
   Want to be in town by six o'clock.

9. Some people crave fo' Memphis Tennessee
   But ol' New Orleans is good enough fo' me.

HAD TO GET UP THIS MORNIN'

REFRAIN

Had to get up this mornin' soon, had to get up this mornin' soon, had to get up this mornin' soon, soon, had to get up this mornin' soon.

FINE

VERSES

'Woke up this mornin' in, such big haste, I
Got up this mornin' an' got up so soon, I
If I I live to see nex' Fall, I

didn't have time to wash my face. Had to
couldn't see nothin' but de stars and moon. Had to
ain't goin drive no mule a - tall. Had to

D.S.

NAW I DON'T

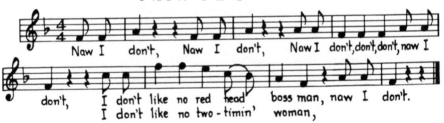

Naw I don't, Naw I don't, Naw I don't, don't, don't, naw I
don't, I don't like no red head boss man, naw I don't.
       I don't like no two - timin' woman,

SCREW THIS COTTON

1. Screw this cotton, screw this cotton, screw this cotton, screw it tight.
2. Work ain't hard boys, Work ain't hard boys, Work ain't hard boys, work ain't hard.
3. Man ain't mean, boys, man ain't mean boys, man ain't mean boys, man ain't mean.
4. Gwine have money, gwine have money, gwine have money, sho's you bo'n.

PO' OL' LAZ'RUS

Po' ol' Laz'rus layin' in be-tween two moun-tains, Po' ol' Laz'rus lay-in' in be-tween two moun-tains, Po' ol' Laz'rus lay-in' in be-tween two moun-tains, Fast a - sleep lawdy fast a - sleep.

VERSES

2. Cap'n tol' de walker "go an' fetch me Laz'rus"
   Cap'n tol' de walker "go an' fetch me Laz'rus"
   Cap'n tol' de walker "go an' fetch me Laz'rus"
   Dead or 'live lawdy dead or 'live.

3. Walker spied ol' Laz'rus layin' in between two mountains
   Walker spied ol' Laz'rus layin' in between two mountains
   Walker spied ol' Laz'rus layin' in between two mountains
   An' he blowed him down, Lawd he blowed him down.

4. Cap'n did you heah 'bout all yo' man goin' leave you
   Cap'n did you heah 'bout all yo' men goin' leave you
   Cap'n did you heah 'bout all yo' men goin' leave you
   Jes because you make yo' day so long.

RAILROAD BILL

1. Railroad Bill, he was so bad, Stole all de money his ol' man had, Wa'n't he bad, Wa'n't he bad, Wa'n't he bad!

2. Railroad Bill, he went down Souf,
   Shot all de teef, out o' de constable's mouf,
   Wa'n't he bad, wa'n't he bad, wa'n't he bad.

3. Railroad Bill, he sat on a fence,
   Called his gal a dirty wench,
   Wa'n't he bad, wa'n't he bad, wa'n't he bad.

4. Railroad Bill, he ran his train so fast
   Couldn't see de postes as dey passed,
   Wa'n't he fast, wa'n't he fast, wa'n't he fast.

LAY TEN DOLLARS DOWN

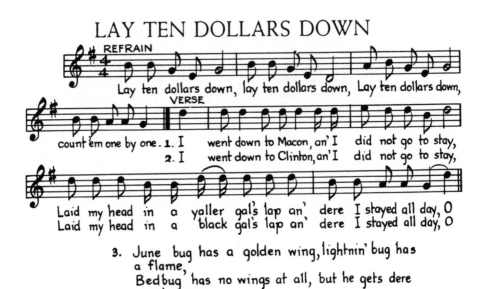

REFRAIN

Lay ten dollars down, lay ten dollars down, Lay ten dollars down, count 'em one by one.

VERSE

1. I went down to Macon, an' I did not go to stay,
   Laid my head in a yaller gal's lap an' dere I stayed all day, O

2. I went down to Clinton, an' I did not go to stay,
   Laid my head in a black gal's lap an' dere I stayed all day, O

3. June bug has a golden wing, lightnin' bug has a flame,
   Bedbug has no wings at all, but he gets dere jes de same.

I GOT A HOUSE IN BALTIMO

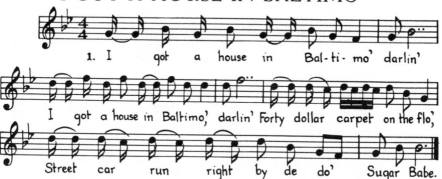

1. I got a house in Bal-ti-mo' darlin'
I got a house in Baltimo,' darlin' Forty dollar carpet on the flo,'
Street car run right by de do' Sugar Babe.

2. What you goin' to do when de meat gives out, darlin'?
What you goin' to do when de meat gives out, darlin'?
What you goin' to do when de meat gives out,
Stan' aroun' de corner with yo' mouth punched out, Sugar Babe.

3. What you goin' to do when de love's all gone, darlin'?
What you goin' to do when de love's all gone, darlin'?
What you goin' to do when de love's all gone,
Stan' aroun' de corner with a great big stone, Sugar Babe.

OL' ELDER BROWN'S

1. Ol' Elder Brown's in town, Ol' Elder Brown's in town ___
Ol' Elder Brown's in town a-with his longcoat on.

2. Ol' Elder Brown tol' Griffin,
"Don't you think I'll win?"
Goin' back to Shreveport Town,
Goin' build my church ag'in.

3. Ol' Elder Brown started his church,
An' de storm blowed it down,
Den Elder sang dis song,
"I'm all out an' down!"

4. He's on de road somewhere,
He's on de road somewhere,
A long tall brownskin man,
He's on de road somewhere.

JOHN HENRY

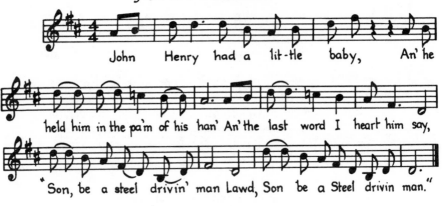

John Henry had a lit-tle baby, An' he held him in the pa'm of his han' An' the last word I heart him say, "Son, be a steel drivin' man Lawd, Son be a Steel drivin man."

2. John Henry was a steel driver,
Ca'ied his hammer all the time.
'Fo' he let that steam drill beat him down,
Die with his hammer in his han' Lawd,
Die with his hammer in his han'!

3. John Henry walked in the tunnel,
An' his Captain by his side,
The rock was so tall, John Henry so small,
He laid down his hammer an' he died, Lawd,
Die with his hammer in his han'!

4. "John Henry tol' his shaker,
Shaker, you had better pray,
If I miss this little piece o' steel,
Tomorrow'll be yo' buryin' day, Lawd,
Tomorrow'll be yo' buryin' day.

5. John Henry said to his captain,
"A man ain't nothin' but a man,
'Fo' I'll let this steam drill beat me down,
I'll die with my hammer in my han' Lawd,
Die with my hammer in my han.

6. That man that hol' that steam drill
Thought he was mighty fine,
John Henry hammered steel, drove ten feet,
While the steam drill only made it nine, Lawd,
While the steam drill only made it nine.

7.   John Henry had a little woman
    An' her name was Polly Ann,
    John Henry said these words to her,
    "Polly, don't love no other man, Lawd,
    Polly don't love no other man!"

8.   John Henry had a little woman
    An' her name was Polly Ann,
    John Henry was an his dyin' bed,
    Polly hammered steel like a man, Lawd,
    Polly hammered steel like a man.

9.   "Who's goin' to shoe your feet?
    Who's goin' to glove your han'?
    Who's goin' to kiss your rosy cheek?
    Who's goin' to be your regular man, Lawd
    Who's goin' to be your regular man?"

10.   "Papa's goin' to shoe my feet,
    Mamma's goin' to glove my hand,
    Sister's goin' to kiss my rose cheek,
    I don't want no regular man, Lawd,
    I don't want no regular man.

11.   John Henry had a little woman,
    The dress she wore was red,
    She got on the track an' never looked back
    She said "I'm goin' where John Henry fell dead," Lawd
    She said "I'm goin' where John Henry fell dead!"

GOIN' KEEP MY SKILLET GREASY

1. O de times is ve - - ry hard, I'm goin'
2. I will go to ol' man' 'Gene's get my -

get me a dimes worth o' lard, I'm goin'
self a sack o' beans,* I'm goin'

keep my skil - let greas - y if I can.
REFRAIN keep my skill - let greas - y if I can.

If I can, can, can, if I can, can, can, I'm goin'

keep my skil - let greas - y if I can.

3. O de rabbit's in de log
   I ain't got no rabbit dog
   Goin' to keep my baby eatin if I can.

* Probably without permission.

VENDOR'S CALL

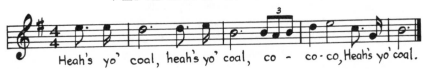

Heah's yo' coal, heah's yo' coal, co - co-co, Heah's yo' coal.

STREET SONG

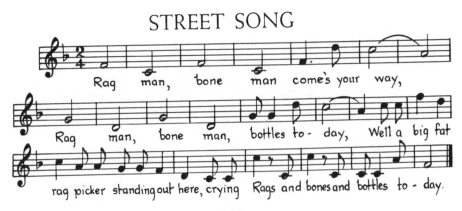

Rag man, bone man come's your way,

Rag man, bone man, bottles to - day, Well a big fat

rag picker standing out here, crying Rags and bones and bottles to - day.

GONNA LEAVE BIG ROCK BEHIND

From the private collection
of André C. Faire

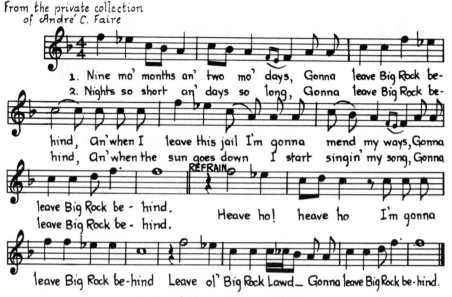

1. Nine mo' months an' two mo' days, Gonna leave Big Rock be-
2. Nights so short an' days so long, Gonna leave Big Rock be-

hind, An' when I leave this jail I'm gonna mend my ways, Gonna
hind, An' when the sun goes down I start singin' my song, Gonna

REFRAIN

leave Big Rock be - hind.
leave Big Rock be - hind.   Heave ho! heave ho I'm gonna

leave Big Rock be-hind Leave ol' Big Rock Lawd— Gonna leave Big Rock be-hind.

3. My gal's waitin' till I get back
Gonna leave Big Rock behind
When I get back gonna "ball de jack"
Gonna leave Big Rock behind.

*The Jefferson County jail in Alabama is commonly called "Big Rock"

WORKIN' ON THE RAILROAD LINE

From the private collection
of André C. Faire

Listen Big Boy if you wanna be a man On the railroad
Listen Big Boy what I hear the people say On the railroad

line. Swingin' Big Boy wid a hammer in yo' han'. Workin' on the railroad
line. Yo' gal's goin' quit you 'cause you never gets no pay. Workin' on the railroad

line. Work on the railroad line, Work on the railroad line,
line. Get you a gal like mine, Get you a gal like mine,

Work on the railroad line, Work-in' on the railroad line.
Get you a gal like mine, Work-in' on the rail-road line.

JIM STRANGE KILLED LULA

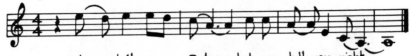

Let me tell you Baby Let me tell you right——
Jim Strange killed Lulu on a Satur-day night——.

2. Seventeen white horses an' a rubber tire hack,
   Carried Lula to the graveyard, but didn't bring her back.

3. Drive slow, Mr. Hearseman, Mr. Hearseman drive slow,
   You carry Lula to the graveyard but won't bring her back no mo'.

WAKE ME

REFRAIN

Wake me Shake me don't let me sleep to late, Got to

get up early in de mornin' Goin' 'to swing on de golden gate.

VERSES

1. Get to de lot be-fo' I do, Catch my mule I'll be there too, Got to
2. Dis ol' gettin' up jes' fo' day, Never did like that thing no way, Got to

get up early in de mornin', Goin' to swing on de gol-den gate.

GOT NO MONEY

Got no money but I will have some Susie——
Daddy sent me to plant a little cotton Susie——

Ain't got no money but I will have some Susie——
O Daddy sent me to plant a little cotton Susie——

246

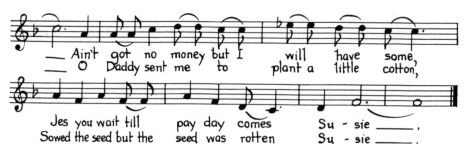

Ain't got no money but I will have some,
Jes you wait till pay day comes Su - sie ____.

O Daddy sent me to plant a little cotton,
Sowed the seed but the seed was rotten Su - sie ____.

ROAD GANG SONG

Pick 'em up   pick 'em up   Let 'em fall down

Dere's a hard rocky bottom   An' she must be foun'.

2. I been on the job so long
   I done lost the use o' my right arm.

3. I worked for the county an' they would not pay
   I worked for the city 'twas the same d__ way.

4. I asked the captain "what time o'day"?
   He got so mad he jes' walked away.

5. I asked for a wheeler but they gave me a plow
   I would make a good "skinner" but I don't know how.

6. You long line "skinners" better learn to "skin"
   Captain Joseph Hobson's got the road agin.

7. I been travelin' long enough to know
   White folks don't love darkies no where you go.

8. I been travelin' for twelve long year
   Never had no trouble till I stopped by here.

247

JUBILEE

Tenor "Lead"

Ju-bi-lee Ju-bi-lee O ___ Lord-y

Baritone Bass

Ju-bi-lee Ju-bi-lee My Lord Ju-bi-lee.

What is the matter the church won't shout O __ Lord-y Some
What is the matter with the mourn--er   The
What is the matter the church don't move   Some

body in there that ought to be out! My Lord Ju-bi-lee.
devils in the "a-men, cor - ner"!
body in there that's carryin'bad news!

LET THE CHURCH ROLL ON

SEBEN TIMES

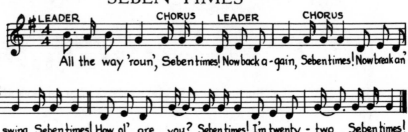

All the way 'roun', Seben times! Now back a-gain, Seben times! Now break an'

swing, Seben times! How ol' are you? Seben times! I'm twenty-two, Seben times!
A piece o' blue, Seben times! Right on yo' shoe, Seben times!
A piece o' red, Seben times! Right on yo' head, Seben times!
A piece o' yeller, Seben times! Right on yo' feller, Seben times!

LULLABY

O mother Glasco where's yo' lamb? I left him down in de

mead-ow. Birds an' de bees singin' in de trees, Po' little lamb say "mammy"

MAMMA DINAH

Mamma Dinah   O ho do mamma Dinah — mamma Dinah   Po' gal I cannot support you
Raggy Eddie   Po' boy Raggy Eddie — Raggy Eddie   Po' boy raggy as a jaybird

O Lawd, Lawd I'll build me a stone fence, O captain Lawd, Lawd I don't want to quit you.

ACKNOWLEDGMENTS

I wish to express my gratitude to the following persons for their inestimable help in making this collection of songs possible: Dr. Charles S. Johnson, Mr. Frederick J. Work, Mr. Edwin R. Embree, Dr. Thomas E. Jones, Dr. Neil C. Van Deusen, Mr. Andre Faire.

BIBLIOGRAPHY

BALLANTA-TAYLOR, C. J. S. *St. Helena Island Spirituals.* New York: Scribners. 1925

BARTON, WILLIAM E. "Hymns of the Slave and the Freedman," *New England Magazine.* 1899
.... *Old Plantation Hymns.* Boston: Lemson Wolffe and Company.

BOATNER, EDWARD, and WILLA TOWNSEND. *Spirituals Triumphant.* Nashville, Tennessee: Sunday School Publishing Board, National Baptist Convention. 1927

BROWN, JOHN M. "Songs of the Slave," *Lippincott's Magazine.* Philadelphia. 1868

BURLIN, NATALIE CURTIS. *Negro Folk Songs.* Hampton Series. Books, I, II Spirituals; Book III, IV Work and Play Songs, Nos. 6716, 6726, 6756, 6766.
"Negro Music at Birth," *The Music Quarterly.* New York. 1919.
"The Negro's Contribution to the Music of America," *The Craftsman.* 1925.

CHRISTY, E. P. *Plantation Melodies.* 1851

CLARK, GEORGE W. *The Libery Minstrel.* New York. 1844.

COLERIDGE-TAYLOR, SAMUEL. *Twenty-four Negro Melodies* (Transcribed for piano). Oliver Ditson Company. Boston. 1905

COUNTEE. *The Imperial Jubilee Sacred Song Book.* 1919.

DETT, R. NATHANIEL. *Religious Jubilee Sacred Song Book.* 1919.

FISHER, WILLIAM ARMS. *Seventy Negro Spirituals.* Boston: Ditson Company. 1926.

GELLERT, LAWRENCE, and ELIE SIEGMEISTER — "Negro Songs of Protest," *American Music League,* New York. 1936.

HALL JOHNSON CHOIR, THE. Notes on the Program of this Organization. 1928.

HANDY, W. C., and ABBE NILES. *Blues: An Anthology.* New York: Albert and Charles Boni. 1926.

HORNBOSTEL, von, E. M. "African Negro Music." *Africa,* Vol. I No. 1, 1928.

HOWARD, J. T. Our *American Music.* New York: J. T. Crowell. 1930.

JACKSON, GEORGE PULLEN. *White Spirituals in the Southern Uplands.* Chapel Hill, North Carolina: The University of North Carolina Press. 1933.

JACKSON, MARYLOU I. *Negro Spirituals and Hymns.* New York: J. Fischer and Brothers. 1935.

JESSYE, EVA. *My Spirituals.* New York: Robbins-Engle. 1927.

JOHNSON, CHARLES S. "Jazz Poetry and Blues," *Carolina Magazine*, Chapel Hill, North Carolina. 1928.

JOHNSON, GUY B. *John Henry*. Chapel Hill, North Carolina: The University of North Carolina Press. 1929.

JOHNSON, J. ROSAMOND, and JAMES WELDON JOHNSON. *The Book of American Negro Spirituals*. New York: The Viking Press. 1925.
.... *Second Book of Negro Spirituals*. New York: The Viking Press. 1925.

Journal of American Folk Lore, The. Vol. 41, No. 162. American Folk Lore Society.

KEMBLE, FRANCES A. *Journal of a Residence on a Georgia Plantation in 1838*. New York: Harper and Brothers. 1863.

KENNEDY, R. EMMETT. *Mellows*. New York: Albert and Charles Boni. 1925.

KING, EDWARD. *Negro Songs and Singers—The Great South*. Hartford, Connecticut: The American Publishing Company. 1875.

KREHBIEL, HENRY E. *Afro-American Folksongs*. New York: G. Schirmer. 1914.

LOCKE, ALAIN. *The New Negro*. New York: Albert and Charles Boni. 1925.

LOMAX, JOHN A. "Sinful Songs of the Southern Negro," *The Music Quarterly*, Vol. XX. New York. 1934.

MARSH, J. B. T. *The Story of the Jubilee Singers: With their Songs.* Boston: Houghton, Mifflin and Company. 1875.

NATIONAL JUBILEE MELODIES. Nashville, Tennessee: The National Baptist Publishing Board.

"NEGRO MUSIC and MINSTRELSY," *The American History and Encyclopedia of Music.* 1910.

ODUM, HOWARD W., and GUY B. JOHNSON. *The Negro and His Songs.* Chapel Hill, North Carolina: The University of North Carolina Press. 1925.

.... Negro Workaday Songs. Chapel Hill, North Carolina: The University of North Carolina Press. 1926.

PARRISH, LYDIA. "The Plantation Songs of Our Old Negro Slaves," *Country Life;* Vol. LXIX. Garden City, New York, Dec. 1935.

PIKE, G. D. The Jubilee Singers of Fisk University. Hoddar and Stoughton. Boston: Lee and Shepard. 1874.

SEWARD, THEODORE. *Jubilee Songs: As Sung by the Jubilee Singers of Fisk University.* New York: Biglow and Main. 1872.

SPEIGHT, W. L. "Notes on South African Native Music," *The Music Quarterly,* Vol. XX. New York. 1934.

"SPIRITUALS ARE PRESERVED," *The New York Sun,* October 24, 1929.

TALLEY, THOMAS W. *Negro Folk Rhymes.* New York: The Macmillan Company. 1922.

WHITE, NEWMAN I. *American Negro Folk Songs.* Cambridge: The University Press. 1928.

WORK, JOHN W., and FREDERICK J. WORK. *Folk Songs of the American Negro.* Nashville, Tennessee: Work Brothers. 1907.

.... New Jubilee Songs. Nashville, Tennessee: Work Brothers. 1901.

WORK, JOHN W. *The Folk Songs of the American Negro.* Nashville, Tennessee: Fisk University Press. 1915.

INDEX OF SONG TITLES

257

259

A CATALOG OF SELECTED DOVER
BOOKS IN ALL FIELDS OF INTEREST

CONCERNING THE SPIRITUAL IN ART, Wassily Kandinsky. Pioneering work by father of abstract art. Thoughts on color theory, nature of art. Analysis of earlier masters. 12 illustrations. 80pp. of text. 5⅜ x 8½. 23411-8 Pa. $4.95

ANIMALS: 1,419 Copyright-Free Illustrations of Mammals, Birds, Fish, Insects, etc., Jim Harter (ed.). Clear wood engravings present, in extremely lifelike poses, over 1,000 species of animals. One of the most extensive pictorial sourcebooks of its kind. Captions. Index. 284pp. 9 x 12. 23766-4 Pa. $14.95

CELTIC ART: The Methods of Construction, George Bain. Simple geometric techniques for making Celtic interlacements, spirals, Kells-type initials, animals, humans, etc. Over 500 illustrations. 160pp. 9 x 12. (USO) 22923-8 Pa. $9.95

AN ATLAS OF ANATOMY FOR ARTISTS, Fritz Schider. Most thorough reference work on art anatomy in the world. Hundreds of illustrations, including selections from works by Vesalius, Leonardo, Goya, Ingres, Michelangelo, others. 593 illustrations. 192pp. 7⅛ x 10¼. 20241-0 Pa. $9.95

CELTIC HAND STROKE-BY-STROKE (Irish Half-Uncial from "The Book of Kells"): An Arthur Baker Calligraphy Manual, Arthur Baker. Complete guide to creating each letter of the alphabet in distinctive Celtic manner. Covers hand position, strokes, pens, inks, paper, more. Illustrated. 48pp. 8¼ x 11. 24336-2 Pa. $3.95

EASY ORIGAMI, John Montroll. Charming collection of 32 projects (hat, cup, pelican, piano, swan, many more) specially designed for the novice origami hobbyist. Clearly illustrated easy-to-follow instructions insure that even beginning papercrafters will achieve successful results. 48pp. 8¼ x 11. 27298-2 Pa. $3.50

THE COMPLETE BOOK OF BIRDHOUSE CONSTRUCTION FOR WOODWORKERS, Scott D. Campbell. Detailed instructions, illustrations, tables. Also data on bird habitat and instinct patterns. Bibliography. 3 tables. 63 illustrations in 15 figures. 48pp. 5¼ x 8½. 24407-5 Pa. $2.50

BLOOMINGDALE'S ILLUSTRATED 1886 CATALOG: Fashions, Dry Goods and Housewares, Bloomingdale Brothers. Famed merchants' extremely rare catalog depicting about 1,700 products: clothing, housewares, firearms, dry goods, jewelry, more. Invaluable for dating, identifying vintage items. Also, copyright-free graphics for artists, designers. Co-published with Henry Ford Museum & Greenfield Village. 160pp. 8¼ x 11. 25780-0 Pa. $10.95

HISTORIC COSTUME IN PICTURES, Braun & Schneider. Over 1,450 costumed figures in clearly detailed engravings–from dawn of civilization to end of 19th century. Captions. Many folk costumes. 256pp. 8⅜ x 11¾. 23150-X Pa. $12.95

THE INFLUENCE OF SEA POWER UPON HISTORY, 1660–1783, A. T. Mahan. Influential classic of naval history and tactics still used as text in war colleges. First paperback edition. 4 maps. 24 battle plans. 640pp. 5⅜ x 8½. 25509-3 Pa. $14.95

THE STORY OF THE TITANIC AS TOLD BY ITS SURVIVORS, Jack Winocour (ed.). What it was really like. Panic, despair, shocking inefficiency, and a little heroism. More thrilling than any fictional account. 26 illustrations. 320pp. 5⅜ x 8½. 20610-6 Pa. $8.95

FAIRY AND FOLK TALES OF THE IRISH PEASANTRY, William Butler Yeats (ed.). Treasury of 64 tales from the twilight world of Celtic myth and legend: "The Soul Cages," "The Kildare Pooka," "King O'Toole and his Goose," many more. Introduction and Notes by W. B. Yeats. 352pp. 5⅜ x 8½. 26941-8 Pa. $8.95

BUDDHIST MAHAYANA TEXTS, E. B. Cowell and Others (eds.). Superb, accurate translations of basic documents in Mahayana Buddhism, highly important in history of religions. The Buddha-karita of Asvaghosha, Larger Sukhavativyuha, more. 448pp. 5⅜ x 8½. 25552-2 Pa. $12.95

ONE TWO THREE . . . INFINITY: Facts and Speculations of Science, George Gamow. Great physicist's fascinating, readable overview of contemporary science: number theory, relativity, fourth dimension, entropy, genes, atomic structure, much more. 128 illustrations. Index. 352pp. 5⅜ x 8½. 25664-2 Pa. $8.95

ENGINEERING IN HISTORY, Richard Shelton Kirby, et al. Broad, nontechnical survey of history's major technological advances: birth of Greek science, industrial revolution, electricity and applied science, 20th-century automation, much more. 181 illustrations. ". . . excellent . . ."–*Isis.* Bibliography. vii + 530pp. 5⅜ x 8¼. 26412-2 Pa. $14.95

DALÍ ON MODERN ART: The Cuckolds of Antiquated Modern Art, Salvador Dalí. Influential painter skewers modern art and its practitioners. Outrageous evaluations of Picasso, Cézanne, Turner, more. 15 renderings of paintings discussed. 44 calligraphic decorations by Dalí. 96pp. 5⅜ x 8½. (USO) 29220-7 Pa. $4.95

ANTIQUE PLAYING CARDS: A Pictorial History, Henry René D'Allemagne. Over 900 elaborate, decorative images from rare playing cards (14th–20th centuries): Bacchus, death, dancing dogs, hunting scenes, royal coats of arms, players cheating, much more. 96pp. 9¼ x 12¼. 29265-7 Pa. $12.95

MAKING FURNITURE MASTERPIECES: 30 Projects with Measured Drawings, Franklin H. Gottshall. Step-by-step instructions, illustrations for constructing handsome, useful pieces, among them a Sheraton desk, Chippendale chair, Spanish desk, Queen Anne table and a William and Mary dressing mirror. 224pp. 8⅛ x 11¼. 29338-6 Pa. $13.95

THE FOSSIL BOOK: A Record of Prehistoric Life, Patricia V. Rich et al. Profusely illustrated definitive guide covers everything from single-celled organisms and dinosaurs to birds and mammals and the interplay between climate and man. Over 1,500 illustrations. 760pp. 7½ x 10⅛. 29371-8 Pa. $29.95

Prices subject to change without notice.

Available at your book dealer or write for free catalog to Dept. GI, Dover Publications, Inc., 31 East 2nd St., Mineola, N.Y. 11501. Dover publishes more than 500 books each year on science, elementary and advanced mathematics, biology, music, art, literary history, social sciences and other areas.